# HOMESIDE
## ACTIVITIES

**GRADE 6**

DEVELOPMENTAL STUDIES CENTER

DEVELOPMENTAL STUDIES CENTER
2000 Embarcadero, Suite 305
Oakland, CA 94606
(510) 533-0213
(800) 666-7270

ISBN 1-57621-149-5
Printed in Canada

# Acknowledgments

Homeside Activities are the product of many people—
thousands of parents, teachers, and children in San Ramon,
Hayward, San Francisco, Cupertino, and Salinas, California;
Louisville, Kentucky; Miami and Homestead, Florida; and
White Plains, New York, who piloted them as part of their
association over the past decade with the Child Development
Project—and the staff people at Developmental Studies
Center who conceived, wrote, and edited them.

Marilyn Watson, Director of the Child Development Project,
has been working with these ideas for years, convinced of the
many valuable ways Homeside Activities could bring parents,
teachers, and children together. She and Eric Schaps,
President of Developmental Studies Center, have made it
possible for this work to go forward. Cindy Litman and her
children Tristan, Toby, Ethan, and Rhiannon Guevin were the
core of the creative team that developed these activities.
Activities were also written by Marilyn Watson, Rosa
Zubizaretta, Lynn Murphy, Anne Goddard, and Carolyn
Hildebrandt. Sylvia Kendzior led a team of staff developers
who helped teachers use the activities in their classrooms
and collected feedback from them. Anne Goddard and Lynn
Murphy edited the materials, Rosa Zubizarreta translated
them into Spanish, and Emily Bezar was the project's desktop
publisher. Additional editorial help was provided by OSO
Publishing Services. Art direction was by Visual Strategies
and Allan Ferguson, the cover illustration by Bud Peen.

We would like to thank the following organizations for their
generous support of the development of *Homeside Activities:*

The William and Flora Hewlett Foundation
The Annenberg Foundation
The Robert Wood Johnson Foundation
Anonymous Donor
Evelyn and Walter Haas, Jr. Fund

# TABLE OF CONTENTS HOMESIDE
### ACTIVITIES

# A Simple Parent-Teacher Partnership for Kids

No matter who you ask, you won't get an argument about whether parents should be involved in their children's education—but you won't get many suggestions for a simple, inclusive way to make it happen, either. That's why Homeside Activities are so powerful. They provide a low-key, nonthreatening way for teachers and parents to build partnerships for kids.

These short, concrete activities in English and Spanish foster communication between teachers and parents and between parents and children. They make it easy for parents to contribute a "homeside" to their children's schoolside learning. And they make it easy for children to "schedule" personal time with a parent or other caretaking adult.

Implicit in the design of Homeside Activities is a message of respect for the diversity of children's families and communities. All activities build on the value for parents and children of talking with each other and listening to each other—in their home language. The activities recognize the social capital of the relationships children go home to when the dismissal bell rings every day. It's important for children to know that the adults guiding them at home are valued by the adults guiding them at school.

Homeside Activities are introduced once or twice a month in class, completed at home, and then incorporated into a follow-up classroom activity or discussion. Typically these 15- to 20-minute activities are reciprocal parent-child interviews or opportunities to share experiences and opinions. The activities are organized by grade level, but none of them have grade-specific references; they can also be used in mixed-grade and ungraded classrooms. The activity topics relate to academic, social, or citizenship themes that are integral to the life of almost any classroom.

For example, in a "Family Folklore" activity for fifth-graders, children learn about their own history while they collect family stories at home; then they contribute to the classroom community by sharing some of these stories in class. One classroom using this activity learned about a runaway slave who lived among the Seminoles, a courtship in which a borrowed Lincoln Continental became a neighborhood attraction, and an extended-family band that serves up the entertainment for family weddings. These seemingly small pieces of information make a big difference in how children and teachers view each other in the classroom.

## BENEFITS OF HOMESIDE ACTIVITIES

|  | FOR STUDENTS | FOR TEACHERS | FOR PARENTS |
|---|---|---|---|
| **Academic/ Intellectual** | • chance to "schedule" time with parent or other adult<br>• build commitment to learning<br>  - engage interest of parent<br>  - see importance and relevance of learning to adult life<br>• build literacy<br>  - communicate clearly<br>  - compare information<br>  - compare points of view<br>  - think abstractly<br>• rehearse school learning<br>• reinforce school learning<br>• reinforce value of home language | • students more invested in academics because of adult involvement<br>• more ways to connect new learning for students<br>  - more aware of students' experiences<br>  - more aware of students' knowledge<br>• opportunity to inform parents of classroom learning program<br>• opportunity to encourage use of home language | • fail-safe way to contribute to child's school learning<br>• exposure to classroom learning approach<br>• exposure to classroom learning topics<br>• opportunity to enjoy child's thinking<br>• opportunity to reinforce importance and relevance of learning<br>• opportunity to reinforce value of home language |
| **Citizenship** | • chance to "schedule" time with parent or other adult<br>• build commitment to values<br>  - engage interest of parent<br>  - see importance and relevance of values to adult life<br>• build complex understanding of values<br>  - compare information<br>  - compare points of view<br>  - think abstractly<br>• reinforce school learning | • students more conscious of values<br>• students more open to examining their behavior<br>• students more likely to see similarities between home and school values | • exposure to citizenship focus of classroom<br>• low-key way to explore child's values<br>• opportunity to communicate personal values<br>• more information for ongoing guidance of child |
| **Classroom Community** | • see parents as valued contributors to classroom<br>• build interpersonal understanding<br>  - of individuals<br>  - of diverse families/situations<br>• build shared learning orientation | • more understanding and empathy<br>  - for individual students<br>  - for parents' hopes and concerns<br>  - for diverse circumstances of students<br>• more comfort inviting parents into community<br>• reinforce shared learning orientation | • more knowledge of child's classroom<br>• more comfort with child's classroom<br>• more comfort with child's teacher<br>• opportunity to contribute to the life of the classroom<br>• low-risk forum for communicating with teacher |

Perhaps as important as the activity-specific information generated by Homeside Activities are the open-ended comments to teachers that parents are encouraged to write. Sometimes the remarks let the teacher in on a child's concerns, for example, about teasing or a bully; sometimes they are simply observations, such as, "Carlos loves science this year"; and sometimes they comment on the value of the activity, as in the following:

> "Allison liked this one. It got us both thinking and she shared more of the day's activities with me."

> "Tyrone says he likes doing these activities because 'your parents can help you' and because it makes you 'think about things.' I think the time spent is very special for him because we always seem to learn something about each other."

> "It was a good way to have a conversation with my son. I am grateful to you for the idea."

Of course some parents might be unable or unwilling to do the activities, in which case it may be possible to find a grandparent, older sibling, neighbor, or staff member who can be a child's regular Homeside partner. For most parents, however, as uncertain as they may be about how to help their children in school, more involvement is welcome when it is introduced through specific activities within their experience and competence. Homeside Activities provide such a structure.

The particular strengths of Homeside Activities fall into three areas: academic and intellectual, citizenship, and classroom community. The chart on page 2 shows how children, teachers, and parents can all benefit in each of these areas.

## Academic and Intellectual Benefits

Homeside Activities contribute to children's academic and intellectual growth in a variety of ways—most directly by providing a motivating context for children to make connections between home and school learning. Children practice critical thinking and communication skills in every activity.

**Motivates Children.** Children can be expected to have a stronger investment in school and academic work if it is an investment made by their parents as well. When children have a Homeside Activity to complete, they can, in effect, schedule a parent's attention and involvement.

**Includes All Parents.** Because the activities engage parents around universal experiences—of growing up, of having opinions, of having adult perspectives on things children are learning—the activities are inclusive and no parent need feel intimidated or incapable of contributing.

"It was a good way to have a conversation with my son."

**Values Home Languages.** For families whose home language is not English, the activities send the message that the school values communication in the home language. For Spanish-speakers this message is explicit since the activities are available in Spanish. For those with home languages other than Spanish or English, students will have gone over the activities in class and will be prepared to serve as "activity directors" at home.

**Promotes Literacy and Thinking Skills.** In doing these activities children practice literacy and thinking skills of talking, listening, synthesizing information to report to parents or back to the classroom, and comparing and evaluating information and points of view—skills that are core competencies for academic and life success.

**Educates Parents about a "Thinking" Curriculum.** Many parents were educated at a time when memorization and rote learning were the primary goals of schooling. Homeside Activities can introduce these parents to a "thinking" curriculum that asks open-ended questions and encourages problem solving and divergent thinking. Rather than limiting parents' role to one of monitoring homework completion, for example, Homeside Activities invite parents to participate in their children's learning experiences and allow them to enjoy their children's ideas and thought processes.

**Makes Children's Past Experiences and Prior Knowledge More Accessible to the Teacher.** Homeside Activities bring new areas of children's experience into the classroom, broadening the possible connections teachers can help children make when they are constructing new knowledge. When teachers and children have widely different background experiences, this can be especially important.

## Citizenship Benefits

Many Homeside Activities involve children and parents in discussions of ethical behavior and principled choices about how to treat oneself and others. The activities provide parents and children with a comfortable way to exchange ideas about important values in their family.

**Deepens Children's Ethical Commitment.** When ethical concerns such as ways we treat a friend or how we identify "heroes" are raised at school and reinforced at home, children see their parents and teachers as partners for their ethical development. Children respond positively when the most important adults in their lives demonstrate congruent investment in their growth as kind and principled human beings.

**Strengthens Children's Development as Decision Makers.** The time children spend thinking about and discussing citizenship goals and ethical concerns helps them build complex understanding of these issues and prepares them to become autonomous, ethical decision makers. Homeside Activities provide a way for children to anticipate ethical choices and rehearse future behaviors.

Children practice critical thinking and communication skills in every activity

**Enhances Parental Guidance.** When parents and children can exchange ideas about citizenship goals and ethical concerns in the context of Homeside Activities, rather than in response to an immediate problem, the discussion can be less loaded for both. In such a context, children may be more likely to let parents into their sometimes mysterious world, and parents may welcome a conversational approach for transmitting their values.

## Classroom Community Benefits

Homeside Activities structure a way to build children's and parents' personal connections to the classroom—to create a shared feeling of community.

**Invites Parents into the Community.** Homeside Activities are invitations to parents to learn more about the life of their children's classroom. They are also a way for parents to become comfortable communicating with their children's teacher.

**Encourages Parents to Contribute Directly to the Life of the Classroom.** Information that parents contribute to the classroom through Homeside Activities deepens students' understanding of each other, provides teachers with insights into children's diverse family situations, and models the school's respect for the home cultures and family experiences of all students. At the same time, Homeside Activities do not require parents who are too busy, too tired, or too embarrassed to be anyplace other than at home with their child when making their contributions.

**Reinforces a Learning Orientation.** A classroom community is defined by the shared goals of its members. Homeside Activities, by virtue of their content and approach, make it clear to everyone involved with the classroom that its members are learning about learning, learning about ethical behavior, and learning about how to treat one another respectfully.

## How These Activities Were Developed

Homeside Activities have been piloted and field-tested in the hundreds of classrooms across the country that have participated in the Child Development Project (CDP), a comprehensive school change effort to help elementary schools become inclusive, caring communities and stimulating, supportive places to learn. Our research has identified several conditions that children need to reach their fullest social and academic potential:

- close and caring relationships with their peers and teachers;
- opportunities to practice and benefit from prosocial values;
- compelling, relevant curriculum; and
- close cooperation and communication between families and school.

A comfortable way to exchange ideas about important values

Homeside Activities are one of the many approaches CDP has developed to meet these conditions, and over the past decade that the Homeside Activities have been used in CDP schools, we have discovered many ways to make them easier for teachers to justify academically, easier for *all* parents to respond to, and "friendlier" for kids to bring home.

## FIELD-TEST FEEDBACK

Feedback from teachers, parents, and students about all aspects of Homeside Activities, coupled with our own classroom and home observations, led us to strengthen and highlight many aspects of the program, especially the following:

1. Provide teachers with introductory and follow-up classroom activities that help them incorporate the Homeside Activities into their academic programs.

2. Make the academic relevance of the activities clear to parents.

3. Make no demands in the activities that might require any resources that could exclude parents from participating.

4. Streamline the amount of information provided to parents, and use simple vocabulary and syntax.

5. Make clear that the activities are voluntary and should be enjoyable.

6. Make clear that the activities are open-ended and not "tests" of children's academic performance or ability.

7. Emphasize the importance of not grading the activities or penalizing students who are unable to return them.

8. Allow at least a week for completion of the activities.

9. Represent diverse cultures in the activity poems, quotes, songs, and other references.

10. Screen all activities for cultural sensitivity.

## Guidelines for Teachers

All Homeside Activities are built around parent-child conversations and usually involve students in a short drawing or writing activity. The activities for grades K–3 are addressed to adults, and adults direct the conversation; the activities for grades 4–5 are addressed to students and are student-directed. To increase both parents' and children's comfort and success in using the activities, consider the following guidelines.

**Introduce the Activities Early in the Year.** During back-to-school night or a similar beginning-of-the-year occasion, personally and enthusiastically inform parents about the purpose and benefits of Homeside Activities—this definitely enhances parents' responsiveness when their children begin bringing home these assignments. If you use the first Homeside Activity in your grade-level set, "Introducing Homeside Activities," it also explains the nature of these assignments. In addition to or instead of "Introducing Homeside Activities," you might send a letter to your students' parents to explain your goals for the activities (see, for example, "A Note about Homeside Activities" on page 9). And as new children enroll in your class, be sure to communicate with their parents about your Homeside Activities program.

**Explain What the Activities Are and What They Are Not.** Most parents appreciate these activities and enjoy the time spent with their children, but you may also meet with some resistance from parents who misunderstand them. To preclude some possible objections, it is important to present the activities in such a way that they don't appear to be a prescription for "fixing" families or for teaching parents how to communicate with their children. Be prepared to speak with parents who expect traditional homework assignments: some may need to understand that this is "real" homework, because conversation is as important to their child's development as are other assignments. Above all, emphasize that these are supposed to be enjoyable, not a burden to either the parents or the children.

**Encourage Parents to Use Their Home Language.** Be sure parents understand that it's perfectly fine for them to do these activities in their home language. Point out the value to their children of developing facility in their home language as well as in English.

**Use Homeside Activities Often.** To see that these assignments are viewed neither as a burden nor a novelty, use them frequently enough for parents and students to see them as an integral part of the classroom program (ideally, one or two times per month). When scheduling their use, keep in mind two considerations: allow families one full week to complete each activity, preferably including a weekend; also coordinate with other teachers so that a family isn't inundated by having all their children bring these activities home at the same time.

**Adjust Your Own Homework Habits.** Make it clear to students (as well as their parents) that these Homeside Activities do not increase their homework load, but are part of it. This may mean that you have to adjust your own homework plans so that these activities are assigned instead of, rather than in addition to, a typical assignment.

**Help Students Engage Family Members.** Treat Homeside Activities with the same seriousness you use for other homework, but do not penalize students when circumstances beyond their control make it impossible or counterproductive to complete an activity. If possible, help students find ways around obstacles they may encounter; when a parent is not available, for example,

**Homeside Activities link children's school and home lives**

encourage students to enlist the participation of other older family members or other older people. You might also have students brainstorm ways to encourage their family's participation, such as thinking ahead to when might be the best time to introduce an activity—not, for example, the night before the assignment is due, or as parents are rushing to get to work or to get dinner on the table.

**Review or Rehearse the Activities in Class.** All the activities are accompanied by ideas for introducing them in class and reviewing what it is that students will be doing at home. Students will feel more confident doing Homeside Activities when they have had a chance to practice or review them first. For example, when the activity asks students to interview their parents, you might have them first ask you or a partner the interview questions. In this way, students will already have an idea of what to say when they begin their dialogue with their parents; also, if their parents are not proficient in English, then the children will "know" how the assignment is supposed to go and can help their parents carry it out. Also, many teachers report that previewing the activity "jump-starts" students' enthusiasm for doing it at home.

**Have Fun!** Again, in considering these guidelines and planning a program of Homeside Activities, remember that flexibility and fun are key to making them work. No one needs to look for the "right" answers to questions, for the "right" conversation to take place, for the "right" products to be returned to class. Instead, the purpose and benefits of Homeside Activities are broader and perhaps more ambitious: to encourage family interactions that link children's school and home lives. We hope you will enjoy these rewarding connections among school, home, students, parents, and teachers.

## Dear Family Members and Family Friends,

Welcome to Homeside Activities! Your child will bring these home to do with you once or twice a month—to add a "homeside" to the "schoolside" learning we are doing in class. These 15- to 20-minute activities

- are built around conversations between you and your child,
- deal with topics and ideas related to your child's schoolwork;
- may involve your child in a short writing or drawing activity, and
- help create a partnership between school and home.

You will find that in Homeside Activities there are no "right" or "wrong" answers, no right or wrong ways to do the activities. You can take the conversation in any direction you want, and you can have as many family members participate as you'd like. Just having these conversations is what counts, because they help your child develop thinking and language skills for life. These assignments contribute to your child's academic and social learning because

- they help you stay in touch with your child's learning;
- working with you increases your child's interest in the work;
- your child gets to practice communication skills and think about important ideas; and
- your child learns from you and sees how school learning relates to "real life."

These don't take long to do, and I'll try to give you plenty of time to fit them into your schedule. Also, teachers will plan together when to use these activities. That way, if you have several children at school, they won't all bring these home at the same time.

Thanks for taking the time to share these wonderful learning experiences with us. I hope you and your child enjoy Homeside Activities.

Your child's teacher,

## Estimados padres, familiares y amigos:

¡Bienvenidos a las Actividades Familiares! Su hija o su hijo traerá estas actividades a casa una o dos veces al mes, para realizarlas junto con Uds. Esto le añadirá una dimensión hogareña a nuestro aprendizaje escolar. Cada actividad requiere de 15 a 20 minutos. En su conjunto, las actividades

- reconocen la importancia fundamental del diálogo familiar;
- tratan ideas y temas relacionados al trabajo escolar de su hija o de su hijo;
- con frecuencia incluyen una breve actividad de dibujo o de escritura y
- ayudan a crear una mejor colaboración entre la escuela y el hogar.

Encontrará que no hay respuestas "correctas" ni "incorrectas" a las Actividades Familiares, ni tampoco maneras correctas o incorrectas de llevarlas a cabo. Puede orientar el diálogo en la dirección que guste, y solicitar la participación de todos los miembros de la familia que desee. Lo importante es el simple hecho de tener estas conversaciones en el idioma que Ud. domina, ya que ésa es la mejor manera de guiar a su hija o a su hijo y de ayudarle a desarrollar su capacidad de razonar. Si su hija o su hijo aprende a comunicarse bien en el idioma del hogar, esto le ayudará a dominar con mayor facilidad el idioma de la escuela. Y el hablar bien dos idiomas le será una gran ventaja a lo largo de su vida.

Estas tareas familiares apoyan el aprendizaje académico y social , ya que:

- le ayudan a Ud. a estar al tanto de lo que su hija o su hijo está aprendiendo en la escuela;
- el trabajar con Ud. despierta el interés de su hija o de su hijo por los trabajos escolares;
- su hija o su hijo puede ejercer sus habilidades de comunicación y pensar acerca de ideas significativas;
- su hija o su hijo aprende de Ud., y puede darse cuenta de cómo lo que aprende en la escuela se relaciona con la vida cotidiana.

Las actividades no le llevarán demasiado tiempo, y trataré de darles un buen plazo en el cual las podrán cumplir. Las maestras también coordinarán el uso de las actividades entre sí, para evitar que, si usted tiene varios niños en la misma escuela, todos le traigan actividades a casa a la misma vez.

Le agradezco el que se tome el trabajo de compartir estos valiosos momentos de aprendizaje con nosotros. Espero que disfruten las Actividades Familiares.

Atentamente,

# Introducing Homeside Activities

### Before Sending Home the Activity

Introduce students to Homeside Activities and have a class discussion about how these activities are different from other homework assignments. Ask students to talk with a partner about what they think they will enjoy about doing Homeside Activities with a parent or adult friend, and what might be hard about doing Homeside Activities.

Have students design covers for Homeside Activity folders on manila folders or envelopes. Send the folders home with the first Homeside Activity. Have students keep completed Homeside Activities in their folders, until they bring the folders and completed activities home again with the final Homeside Activity of the year.

### Follow-Up

Have students share their reactions to the first Homeside Activity. What did they enjoy about the activity? What did their parent or adult friend enjoy? What problems did students encounter? What was most interesting about the activity? Most surprising? Give students a chance to show and explain their pictures to their partners or to the class.

# Introducing Homeside Activities

### Dear Student,

*You are in charge of this Homeside Activity, which means you are in charge of finding an adult to do it with you, finding time you both have free to do it, explaining and "directing" the activity, making sure the adult signs it, and bringing it back to class. Please find about 20 minutes that you can spend on the activity with a parent or other adult—a neighbor, grandparent, older brother or sister, or family friend. If you'd like, get a bunch of people involved!*

*One of the most important reasons for doing this activity is that you and the adult will learn things from each other about what you think, feel, know, and want to know. In class we can then also learn from each other, when we share what we have learned at home. Just be sure to ask the adults for permission to pass along what they say—and don't forget to thank them for contributing to our class's learning!*

Tell a parent or other adult that you will be bringing home some Homeside Activities this year.

Explain that these activities ask you to talk with a parent or other adult about topics connected to your class work. Show the adult the folder you made for your Homeside Activities, and explain your design.

Talk with the adult about how the Homeside Activities will be different from other homework. Then tell each other what you might like about having these "homework" conversations.

Take notes on the back of this page.

### NOTES

Ways the Homeside Activities will be different from other homework:

........................................................................................

........................................................................................

........................................................................................

........................................................................................

Some things the adult might like about your "homework" conversations:

........................................................................................

........................................................................................

........................................................................................

........................................................................................

Some things you might like about your "homework" conversations:

........................................................................................

........................................................................................

........................................................................................

........................................................................................

## Comments

After you have completed this activity, each of you please sign your name and the date below. If you have any comments, please write them in the space provided.

## Signatures                                                Date

_____    _____    _____

Please return this activity to school. Thank you.

# Anticipation

### Before Sending Home the Activity

Send this activity home after you have held a start-the-year class meeting or have reviewed with your class what this new school year will entail.

When introducing the activity, talk about the meaning of "anticipation" with students. Also ask the class for suggestions about making this Homeside Activity successful.

### Follow-Up

Have students do partner interviews about their goals and challenges for this school year.

# Anticipation

### Dear Student,

*You are in charge of this Homeside Activity, which means you are in charge of finding an adult to do it with you, finding time you both have free to do it, explaining and "directing" the activity, making sure the adult signs it, and bringing it back to class. Please find about 20 minutes that you can spend on the activity with a parent or other adult—a neighbor, grandparent, older brother or sister, or family friend. If you'd like, get a bunch of people involved!*

*One of the most important reasons for doing this activity is that you and the adult will learn things from each other about what you think, feel, know, and want to know. In class we can then also learn from each other, when we share what we have learned at home. Just be sure to ask the adults for permission to pass along what they say—and don't forget to thank them for contributing to our class's learning!*

Tell a parent or other adult what you anticipate about this school year. What do you think you will enjoy? What do you think might be most challenging, either academically or socially? What will help you meet this challenge?

Then ask your parent or the adult what he or she found challenging in school at your age, either academically or socially. What helped him or her meet this challenge?

Take notes on the back of this page.

### NOTES

What I anticipate enjoying about this school year:

..................................................................................................

..................................................................................................

What I anticipate will be most challenging this school year:

..................................................................................................

..................................................................................................

What could help me meet this challenge:

..................................................................................................

..................................................................................................

What the adult found challenging in school at my age:

..................................................................................................

..................................................................................................

What helped the adult meet the challenge:

..................................................................................................

..................................................................................................

## Comments

After you have completed this activity, each of you please sign your name and the date below. If you have any comments, please write them in the space provided.

..................................................................................................

..................................................................................................

..................................................................................................

..................................................................................................

**Signatures**                                                          **Date**

_____    _____    _____

Please return this activity to school. Thank you.

# Personal Map

### Before Sending Home the Activity

This is a useful getting-to-know-you activity for the beginning of the school year; you could also use it with map-reading units in history or social studies. Explain to students that you want them to make a "personal map"—that is, a map of the places that they frequent or that are personally important to them. Point out the range of possibilities this could include—their bedroom, a certain chair they like to sit in at home, a store they shop in on their way home from school, or any place where they enjoy spending time. Give them an example by naming some of the places that would show up on your personal map, and why, and do a quick sketch of your map on the board.

Have students begin by doing some brainstorming on their own to come up with a list of the places they want to include on their maps. Have them draw a first draft of the map; explain that they don't have to draw the map to scale, but they should try to place their locations correctly in relation to one other. Then have students pair up and interview their partners about their maps—what is on them and why, what questions it raises for the interviewing partner, and so on. Encourage students to explore each other's thinking, as this might help fill out the map or make it more accurate.

Review the Homeside Activity with students, and make sure they bring the final draft of their maps home with them with their activity sheet. Also ask the class for suggestions about making this Homeside Activity successful.

### Follow-Up

Have a whole-class conversation about how the activity went. What was easy or hard about trying to make the map? How did adults at home respond to students' maps? What kinds of things did students and adults have in common on their maps? How do students think their personal maps might change as they get older?

# Personal Map

### Dear Student,

*You are in charge of this Homeside Activity, which means you are in charge of finding an adult to do it with you, finding time you both have free to do it, explaining and "directing" the activity, making sure the adult signs it, and bringing it back to class. Please find about 20 minutes that you can spend on the activity with a parent or other adult—a neighbor, grandparent, older brother or sister, or family friend. If you'd like, get a bunch of people involved!*

*One of the most important reasons for doing this activity is that you and the adult will learn things from each other about what you think, feel, know, and want to know. In class we can then also learn from each other, when we share what we have learned at home. Just be sure to ask the adults for permission to pass along what they say—and don't forget to thank them for contributing to our class's learning!*

Show your personal map to a parent or other adult. Explain why you included each location on your map. Invite the adult's comments and questions about your map.

Then interview the adult about what he or she would include on a personal map. (Invite the adult to make a quick map if that seems helpful.) Find out why the adult would include these locations. Discuss the similarities and differences between the items on your personal maps.

Take notes on the back of the page.

## NOTES

### What the adult would include on a personal map

Place:

.................................................................................................................

Reason for including it:

.................................................................................................................

Place:

.................................................................................................................

Reason for including it:

.................................................................................................................

Place:

.................................................................................................................

Reason for including it:

.................................................................................................................

Place:

.................................................................................................................

Reason for including it:

.................................................................................................................

.................................................................................................................

## Comments

After you have completed
this activity, each of you
please sign your name and
the date below. If you have
any comments, please
write them in the space
provided.

.................................................................................

.................................................................................

.................................................................................

.................................................................................

.................................................................................

**Signatures**                                             **Date**

_____     _____     _____

Please return this activity to school. Thank you.

# It Changed the World

### Before Sending Home the Activity

This activity is useful in conjunction with units in science or social studies about inventions, technology, industrialization, historical events, and the like. Ask students to name inventions that changed the world, and list these on the board—for example, the printing press, antibiotics, automobiles, the atom bomb, the personal computer, and so on. Discuss with students the impact of these inventions, encouraging them to think both globally and personally: not only how these inventions changed the world (for example, economically, environmentally, politically, medically), but also how they affected people's day-to-day lives.

From the list the class has compiled, have students choose the invention they believe has made the greatest impact on people's lives, for better or worse. (You might also give students some time to research their choice, to support and extend their understanding.) Have them note their choices and reasoning on the back of their Homeside Activity page.

Review the activity with the class, perhaps modeling the interview with a student or classroom aide. Also ask the class for suggestions about making this Homeside Activity successful.

### Follow-Up

Make a class timeline of the inventions discussed by students and adults at home. Invite volunteers to describe anything new or interesting they learned from their conversations with the adults. Did they see new benefits or burdens of an invention? After students have had a chance to discuss the activity, ask if the conversation changed anyone's mind about what invention they would choose. Why or why not?

# It Changed the World

### Dear Student,

*You are in charge of this Homeside Activity, which means you are in charge of finding an adult to do it with you, finding time you both have free to do it, explaining and "directing" the activity, making sure the adult signs it, and bringing it back to class. Please find about 20 minutes that you can spend on the activity with a parent or other adult—a neighbor, grandparent, older brother or sister, or family friend. If you'd like, get a bunch of people involved!*

*One of the most important reasons for doing this activity is that you and the adult will learn things from each other about what you think, feel, know, and want to know. In class we can then also learn from each other, when we share what we have learned at home. Just be sure to ask the adults for permission to pass along what they say—and don't forget to thank them for contributing to our class's learning!*

Tell a parent or other adult about the invention you think has had the most impact on people's lives. Explain the reasons for your choice. What would our world be like if it hadn't been invented? How would our lives be better? How might our lives be worse?

Then ask the adult what invention he or she thinks has had the most impact on people's lives. How has that invention affected the adult's life? Given the choice, would the adult rather have this invention in the world, or not?

Take notes on the back of this page.

### NOTES

The invention I think had the greatest impact on people's lives:

..............................................................................................................................

..............................................................................................................................

Why I think so:

..............................................................................................................................

..............................................................................................................................

..............................................................................................................................

..............................................................................................................................

The invention the adult thinks had the greatest impact on people's lives:

..............................................................................................................................

..............................................................................................................................

Reasons and opinions:

..............................................................................................................................

..............................................................................................................................

..............................................................................................................................

..............................................................................................................................

..............................................................................................................................

## Comments

After you have completed this activity, each of you please sign your name and the date below. If you have any comments, please write them in the space provided.

..............................................................................

..............................................................................

..............................................................................

..............................................................................

**Signatures**                                                      **Date**

_____   _____   _____

Please return this activity to school. Thank you.

# Where in the World?

### Before Sending Home the Activity

Use this activity to introduce a geography, history, or social studies unit, to build students' understanding of how these subjects connect to their own curiosity about the world around them. Begin by making a class list of places that students have studied, read about, or seen in films or on television that they found interesting. Ask students why these places interest them, and help them identify any common themes—for instance, scenery, wildlife, history, culture, connection to personal heritage, and so on.

Ask students to choose one place (not necessarily from the list) that they would like to visit—a continent, country, city, wilderness, or other region they would like to explore. Give them time to research the area they have chosen and have them draft a brief essay about what they would want to see or experience on their visit, and why. Have them bring home their final draft with their Home Activity sheet.

Before sending home the activity, make sure students are familiar with how to do Venn diagrams, and review that if necessary. Also ask the class for suggestions about making this Homeside Activity successful.

### Follow-Up

Have a whole-class conversation about how the activity went. Did students get new ideas for interesting places to visit? What were some of the similarities and differences between adult and student choices? Did the adults' interest in places fit the common themes students had identified in their own choices? Did any new themes emerge? Connect students' ideas about these themes to the new unit of study when you introduce it.

# Where in the World?

**Dear Student,**

*You are in charge of this Homeside Activity, which means you are in charge of finding an adult to do it with you, finding time you both have free to do it, explaining and "directing" the activity, making sure the adult signs it, and bringing it back to class. Please find about 20 minutes that you can spend on the activity with a parent or other adult—a neighbor, grandparent, older brother or sister, or family friend. If you'd like, get a bunch of people involved!*

*One of the most important reasons for doing this activity is that you and the adult will learn things from each other about what you think, feel, know, and want to know. In class we can then also learn from each other, when we share what we have learned at home. Just be sure to ask the adults for permission to pass along what they say—and don't forget to thank them for contributing to our class's learning!*

Talk with a parent or other adult about the place you want to visit. Read aloud your essay and answer any questions the adult might have about your interest in that place.

Then ask the adult to name a place that they would like to visit. Ask the adult to explain his or her interest in this place. What would he or she like to do there? Why? What would he or she expect to see there? Discuss the similarities and differences between the places you have chosen and the reasons for your choices.

Take notes by writing your and the adult's reasons on the Venn diagram on the back of the page.

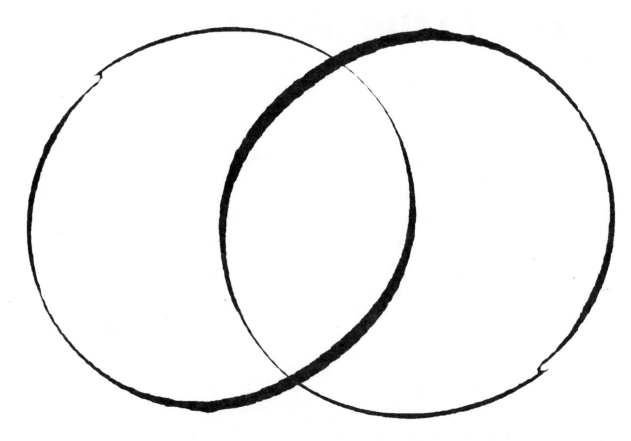

Why I Want to Go to .........................................

Why the Adult Wants to Go to .........................................

.....................................................................................................

## Comments

After you have completed this activity, each of you please sign your name and the date below. If you have any comments, please write them in the space provided.

**Signatures**

**Date**

_____     _____

Please return this activity to school. Thank you.

# Personal Poetry

### Before Sending Home the Activity

Use this activity when your students are working with poetry as part of their writing curriculum, or on its own to introduce poetry to your class.

Discuss with students what they think of poetry. Have they read much? Do they like it? What do they think poets write about? Do they think writing poetry is difficult?

Then read aloud the following poem to the class:

### Expression of Feelings

Only be willing to search for poetry, and there will be poetry:
My soul, a tiny speck, is my tutor.
Evening sun and fragrant grass are common things,
But, with understanding, they can become glorious verse.
—*Mei Yüan**

Invite students' response to the poem. Do they think poetry is always an expression of feelings? Do they think common things are a good place to search for poetry?

Reread the poem, including the title, and ask students to think about where they would search if they wanted to write a poem. Encourage them to be as free as possible in their thinking—would they try to understand an everyday sight or experience, a daydream or goal, a feeling or person? Give them examples of your own, and give reasons for your ideas.

Have each student list several different things he or she might write a poem about and then choose one to note, along with their reasons, on the back of their Homeside Activity sheet. Review the activity with them and ask for suggestions about making this Homeside Activity successful.

"Expression of Feelings VII" by Yüan Mei (4 lines, p. 69) from *The Penguin Book of Chinese Verse: Verse Translations by Robert Kotewall and Norman L. Smith,* edited by A. R. Davis (Penguin Books, 1962). Translation copyright © N. L. Smith and R. H. Kotewall, 1962.

## Follow-Up

Invite volunteers to describe how the activity went at home. Did adults give ideas that surprised or intrigued students? Did they find that some adults *have* written poems? What about?

Have students write a poem about the subjects they have chosen. Encourage them to think about their subject in many different ways: how it makes them feel, its colors, its personality, its effect on them, and so on. If they need help getting started, give them sentence prompts to start their poems, such as:

My poem is about _____
because _____.

When I see _____,
I think of _____.

I feel _____.

For further ideas about introducing students to poetry, see *Let's Do a Poem: Introducing Poetry to Children*, by Nancy Larrick; *Rose, Where Did You Get That Red?* by Kenneth Koch; *Knock at a Star: A Child's Introduction to Poetry*, by X. J. Kennedy and Dorothy M. Kennedy; or any other of the many fine guides available for using poetry with children.

# Personal Poetry

### Dear Student,

*You are in charge of this Homeside Activity, which means you are in charge of finding an adult to do it with you, finding time you both have free to do it, explaining and "directing" the activity, making sure the adult signs it, and bringing it back to class. Please find about 20 minutes that you can spend on the activity with a parent or other adult—a neighbor, grandparent, older brother or sister, or family friend. If you'd like, get a bunch of people involved!*

*One of the most important reasons for doing this activity is that you and the adult will learn things from each other about what you think, feel, know, and want to know. In class we can then also learn from each other, when we share what we have learned at home. Just be sure to ask the adults for permission to pass along what they say—and don't forget to thank them for contributing to our class's learning!*

Read the poem "Expression of Feelings" (on the other side of the page) aloud to a parent or other adult. Describe the conversation you and your classmates had about what the poet is saying—that a poem can be an expression of your feelings for any common thing or experience, person or place, dream or goal.

Then tell the adult about the subject you have chosen for a poem. Explain the reasons for your choice. Ask the adult what he or she might write a poem about, and why.

Take notes on the back of this page. In class, we will turn our ideas into poetry.

## Expression of Feelings

Only be willing to search for poetry, and there will be poetry:

My soul, a tiny speck, is my tutor.

Evening sun and fragrant grass are common things,

But, with understanding, they can become glorious verse.

—*Mei Yüan**

"Expression of Feelings VII" by Yüan Mei (4 lines, p. 69) from *The Penguin Book of Chinese Verse: Verse Translations by Robert Kotewall and Norman L. Smith,* edited by A. R. Davis (Penguin Books, 1962). Translation copyright © N. L. Smith and R. H. Kotewall, 1962.

What I think would be a good subject for a poem:

..............................................................................................................................................

My reasons:

..............................................................................................................................................

..............................................................................................................................................

..............................................................................................................................................

What the adult would write a poem about:

..............................................................................................................................................

The adult's reasons:

..............................................................................................................................................

..............................................................................................................................................

..............................................................................................................................................

## Comments

After you have completed this activity, each of you please sign your name and the date below. If you have any comments, please write them in the space provided.

..............................................................................................................................................

..............................................................................................................................................

..............................................................................................................................................

..............................................................................................................................................

..............................................................................................................................................

**Signatures**                                                                                          **Date**

...................................................          ...................................................          ...................................................

Please return this activity to school. Thank you.

# Full Report

### Before Sending Home the Activity

Use this Home Activity towards the end of a semester, shortly before students receive their report cards. Draw a prototype of a report card on the board or on butcher or chart paper, and give students a minute to look it over. Ask students what they think of the report card: What do they think it shows about how they're doing in school? What doesn't it show? What new categories or kinds of comments could they add to the report card to help show their work, effort, and progress? Write students' responses on the board, and after the class discussion ask students to note on the back of their Home Activity sheets the categories or comments they would like to add to their own report cards. (They don't have to stick to the class list—encourage them to add other "personalized" categories that occur to them, as well.)

Before sending home the activity, ask the class for suggestions about making this Homeside Activity successful.

### Follow-Up

Have a whole-class conversation about how the activity went. Invite volunteers to explain the categories or comments that adults at home would like to see added to the report card, and make a list of these on the board. Help students identify any common themes, and discuss with them why adults might find these important.

Make sure students keep their Home Activity sheets, to refer to later. Then when it's time to send home the report cards, have students write an addendum that addresses the "missing" categories they noted on their Home Activity sheet. Also encourage them to address the areas the adult was interested in, if possible.

# Full Report

### Dear Student,

*You are in charge of this Homeside Activity, which means you are in charge of finding an adult to do it with you, finding time you both have free to do it, explaining and "directing" the activity, making sure the adult signs it, and bringing it back to class. Please find about 20 minutes that you can spend on the activity with a parent or other adult—a neighbor, grandparent, older brother or sister, or family friend. If you'd like, get a bunch of people involved!*

*One of the most important reasons for doing this activity is that you and the adult will learn things from each other about what you think, feel, know, and want to know. In class we can then also learn from each other, when we share what we have learned at home. Just be sure to ask the adults for permission to pass along what they say—and don't forget to thank them for contributing to our class's learning!*

Describe to a parent or other adult the conversation you had in class about report cards. What do you and your classmates find useful about them? What do you think report cards don't show about how you are doing in school? Explain to the adult the categories or comments you would like to add to your own report card. Give your reasons for why these would be useful for helping the adult understand how you are doing in school.

Then ask the adult what categories or comments he or she would like to see on the report card. What would the adult like to know about you in school that the report card doesn't show? Why?

Take notes on the back of the page.

## NOTES

Categories or kinds of comments I would like to see on my report card:

........................................................................

........................................................................

........................................................................

My reasons:

........................................................................

........................................................................

........................................................................

Categories or kinds of comments the adult would like to see on my report card:

........................................................................

........................................................................

........................................................................

The adult's reasons:

........................................................................

........................................................................

........................................................................

........................................................................

### Comments
..................

After you have completed
this activity, each of you
please sign your name and
the date below. If you have
any comments, please
write them in the space
provided.

........................................................................

........................................................................

........................................................................

........................................................................

**Signatures**                                                    **Date**

_____     _____     _____

Please return this activity to school. Thank you.

# I Would If I Could

### Before Sending Home the Activity

Use this Home Activity in conjunction with social studies, current events, history, or literature—any subject that raises interesting ideas about what needs to be "fixed" in the world. Ask students to think about what one thing they would change to make the world a better place, if they could. Invite students' ideas and list them on the board, without discussion of their relative merits. Then have students work in pairs and interview each other about what they would change. Encourage them to offer reasons and probe each other's thinking (but make sure they understand that the point isn't to agree on one idea, but just to discuss their different ways of thinking). Have them note their own choices and reasoning on the back of their Home Activity Sheet.

Before sending home the activity, ask the class for suggestions about making this Homeside Activity successful.

### Follow-Up

Have a whole-class conversation about how the activity went. Did anyone get some interesting ideas from the adults? Did many students and their adults agree on what to change in the world? Invite volunteers to explain their adult's ideas, as well.

# I Would If I Could

### Dear Student,

*You are in charge of this Homeside Activity, which means you are in charge of finding an adult to do it with you, finding time you both have free to do it, explaining and "directing" the activity, making sure the adult signs it, and bringing it back to class. Please find about 20 minutes that you can spend on the activity with a parent or other adult—a neighbor, grandparent, older brother or sister, or family friend. If you'd like, get a bunch of people involved!*

*One of the most important reasons for doing this activity is that you and the adult will learn things from each other about what you think, feel, know, and want to know. In class we can then also learn from each other, when we share what we have learned at home. Just be sure to ask the adults for permission to pass along what they say—and don't forget to thank them for contributing to our class's learning!*

Describe to a parent or other adult the conversation you had in class about things you and your classmates would like to change in the world if you could. Explain the one thing you chose, and give reasons for your choice.

Then ask the adult what one thing he or she would change to make the world a better place, if he or she could. Ask the adult to explain this choice. Discuss the similarities and differences between your two choices.

Take notes on the back of the page.

## NOTES

The one thing I would change to make the world a better place:

...................................................................................

...................................................................................

My reasons:

...................................................................................

...................................................................................

...................................................................................

The one thing the adult would change to make the world a better place:

...................................................................................

...................................................................................

The adult's reasons:

...................................................................................

...................................................................................

...................................................................................

...................................................................................

### Comments

After you have completed this activity, each of you please sign your name and the date below. If you have any comments, please write them in the space provided.

...................................................................................

...................................................................................

...................................................................................

...................................................................................

**Signatures**                                                **Date**

_____  _____  _____

Please return this activity to school. Thank you.

# Taking Stock

### Before Sending Home the Activity

Use this activity as part of observing a New Year—the January 1 observance, the Chinese New Year, Jewish New Year, or any other culture's celebration of a similar holiday.

Ask students what they think it means to "take stock." When do people feel the need to take stock of their lives? What do they hope to achieve? Why is the New Year, in many cultures, a time when people often decide to take stock?

Give students some time to take stock of their school year so far. What are they proud of? What do they wish had happened differently? What could they do next time to make it happen differently? Having taken stock, what are their goals for the New Year? Have students write their ideas on the back of the Homeside Activity sheet.

Before sending home the activity, ask the class for suggestions about making this Homeside Activity successful.

### Follow-Up

Have a whole-class conversation about how the activity went. Did many students find that they and the adults shared similar goals for the student's school year? How could students and adults check in with each other about meeting their respective goals? Take stock yourself, and let students know your goals for the new school year, too.

# Taking Stock

## Dear Student,

*You are in charge of this Homeside Activity, which means you are in charge of finding an adult to do it with you, finding time you both have free to do it, explaining and "directing" the activity, making sure the adult signs it, and bringing it back to class. Please find about 20 minutes that you can spend on the activity with a parent or other adult—a neighbor, grandparent, older brother or sister, or family friend. If you'd like, get a bunch of people involved!*

*One of the most important reasons for doing this activity is that you and the adult will learn things from each other about what you think, feel, know, and want to know. In class we can then also learn from each other, when we share what we have learned at home. Just be sure to ask the adults for permission to pass along what they say—and don't forget to thank them for contributing to our class's learning!*

Describe to a parent or other adult the conversation you had in class about the meaning of "taking stock." Explain why you think people take stock, especially at the beginning of a New Year.

Read to the adult the ideas you came up with when you took stock of your school year so far. With the adult, agree on one goal you share for yourself. Then agree on one goal you share for the adult.

Take notes on the back of this page.

## HOMESIDE ACTIVITY

**NOTES**

What I am proud of in this school year so far:

.......................................................................................................................

.......................................................................................................................

What I wish had happened differently:

.......................................................................................................................

.......................................................................................................................

After taking stock, these are my goals for the New Year at school:

.......................................................................................................................

.......................................................................................................................

A New Year's goal for me that the adult and I agree on (this can be same as the goal you chose for yourself, above):

.......................................................................................................................

.......................................................................................................................

A New Year's goal for the adult that the adult and I agree on:

.......................................................................................................................

.......................................................................................................................

........................................................................................................................................

### Comments
....................

After you have completed this activity, each of you please sign your name and the date below. If you have any comments, please write them in the space provided.

.......................................................................

.......................................................................

.......................................................................

.......................................................................

.......................................................................

**Signatures**                                                    **Date**

_____   _____   _____

Please return this activity to school. Thank you.

........................................................................................................................................

# Upgrade

### Before Sending Home the Activity

Use this activity about midway through the year—when students have experience to go on, yet still time to effect change.

Ask students to think about their school year so far. If there was one thing they could change about school in this grade, what would it be? Give students some to time to think about this on their own, or have partners discuss the topic, and then have students note their thinking on the back of their Homeside Activity sheets.

Review the activity with the class, and ask for suggestions about making this Homeside Activity successful.

### Follow-Up

Have a whole-class conversation about students' and adults' answers about what they would change about school. Write their ideas in two lists on the board, one for students' ideas and the other for adults'. Help the class identify similarities and differences between the lists. Are there some things that always seem true for people at their age? Are there some that are quite different between the adult and student lists? What might be the reasons for those differences between generations?

Look at the students' list with the class, and help students identify any situations that they could try to change. Hold class meetings to discuss such cases, and encourage students to come up with realistic solutions. For example, if a lot of students say there's too much homework, that's not about to change—but perhaps they could brainstorm how to manage their time so that they can do their homework and have fun after school. Or if many students dislike a certain school rule, they might discuss the reasons for it and come up with an alternative that addresses those reasons.

# Upgrade

### Dear Student,

*You are in charge of this Homeside Activity, which means you are in charge of finding an adult to do it with you, finding time you both have free to do it, explaining and "directing" the activity, making sure the adult signs it, and bringing it back to class. Please find about 20 minutes that you can spend on the activity with a parent or other adult—a neighbor, grandparent, older brother or sister, or family friend. If you'd like, get a bunch of people involved!*

*One of the most important reasons for doing this activity is that you and the adult will learn things from each other about what you think, feel, know, and want to know. In class we can then also learn from each other, when we share what we have learned at home. Just be sure to ask the adults for permission to pass along what they say—and don't forget to thank them for contributing to our class's learning!*

Ask a parent or other adult to remember back to when he or she was your age. Ask the adult, "If you could have changed one thing about school when you were my age, what would it have been?"

Then tell the adult the one thing you would change about school if you could. Discuss how your answers are similar to or different from the adult's, and why this might be so. If you have any ideas for ways to make the changes you'd like at school, discuss those as well.

Take notes on the back of this page.

### NOTES

What I would change about school if I could:

.................................................................................................

.................................................................................................

My reasons:

.................................................................................................

.................................................................................................

What I could do:

.................................................................................................

.................................................................................................

What the adult would have changed about school when he or she was my age:

.................................................................................................

.................................................................................................

Reasons:

.................................................................................................

.................................................................................................

How our answers are alike and different, and why we think that is:

.................................................................................................

.................................................................................................

## Comments

After you have completed this activity, each of you please sign your name and the date below. If you have any comments, please write them in the space provided.

.................................................................

.................................................................

.................................................................

.................................................................

**Signatures**                                    **Date**

_____    _____    _____

Please return this activity to school. Thank you.

# Good Sports

### Before Sending Home the Activity

Because athletes figure so prominently in our public life and in current events, you might use this activity with a relevant social studies, current events, or literature topic.

Review the activity with the class, and ask for suggestions about making this Homeside Activity successful.

### Follow-Up

Have a whole-class conversation about sports stars as role models. Invite students to name sports stars that they or their adults at home consider present-day role models, and encourage them to explain the reasons behind these choices. What did adults think about sports stars' responsibility to be role models? Do students agree or disagree?

# Good Sports

### Dear Student,

*You are in charge of this Homeside Activity, which means you are in charge of finding an adult to do it with you, finding time you both have free to do it, explaining and "directing" the activity, making sure the adult signs it, and bringing it back to class. Please find about 20 minutes that you can spend on the activity with a parent or other adult—a neighbor, grandparent, older brother or sister, or family friend. If you'd like, get a bunch of people involved!*

*One of the most important reasons for doing this activity is that you and the adult will learn things from each other about what you think, feel, know, and want to know. In class we can then also learn from each other, when we share what we have learned at home. Just be sure to ask the adults for permission to pass along what they say—and don't forget to thank them for contributing to our class's learning!*

Interview a parent or other adult about whether sports stars do or do not have a responsibility to be positive role models. Ask the adult if there was any sports star that he or she admired at your age. Does the adult think there are any sports stars today that are positive role models for young people? Who? Does the adult think sports stars have more responsibility to be good role models than other famous people? Why or why not?

Give your opinions, too, and take notes on the back of this page.

### NOTES

A sports star the adult admired at my age:

........................................................................................

The adult's reasons:

........................................................................................

........................................................................................

........................................................................................

A sports star the adult thinks is a good role model for young people today:

........................................................................................

Reasons:

........................................................................................

........................................................................................

........................................................................................

The adult's opinion on whether or not sports stars have more responsibility to be good role models than other famous people:

........................................................................................

........................................................................................

........................................................................................

........................................................................................

................................................................................................................................

## Comments
..............................

After you have completed this activity, each of you please sign your name and the date below. If you have any comments, please write them in the space provided.

........................................................................................

........................................................................................

........................................................................................

........................................................................................

**Signatures**                                                    **Date**

_____          _____          _____

Please return this activity to school. Thank you.

................................................................................................................................

# What Next?

## Before Sending Home the Activity

You can use this activity any time you want to involve your students in deciding what topic they will study next. You'll notice that the wording on the students' Homeside Activity page is deliberately vague, so that it can be used to refer to study topics in any subject area—science, social studies, history, current events, and so on.

Review the activity with the class, and give students some time to think about what topic they would like to study. You might want to start off with a whole-class conversation to make sure students understand the parameters of their choice, and perhaps a little whole-class brainstorming if students need help getting their thinking started.

Have students note their choice and reasons for it on the back of their Homeside Activity sheet. If the class has been brainstorming, make sure students understand that they aren't limited to the ideas generated during the brainstorming.

Before sending home the activity, ask for suggestions about making this Homeside Activity successful.

## Follow-Up

Hold a class meeting to determine the next study topic. Begin by listing students' ideas on the board; also ask if adults at home had any ideas that students found interesting and would like to add to the list of possibilities. Help students review the list and categorize the ideas (they'll find that many ideas are similar, which will make consensus building easier); then help them discuss their options and arrive at consensus on the topic to be pursued.

# What Next?

**Dear Student,**

*You are in charge of this Homeside Activity, which means you are in charge of finding an adult to do it with you, finding time you both have free to do it, explaining and "directing" the activity, making sure the adult signs it, and bringing it back to class. Please find about 20 minutes that you can spend on the activity with a parent or other adult—a neighbor, grandparent, older brother or sister, or family friend. If you'd like, get a bunch of people involved!*

*One of the most important reasons for doing this activity is that you and the adult will learn things from each other about what you think, feel, know, and want to know. In class we can then also learn from each other, when we share what we have learned at home. Just be sure to ask the adults for permission to pass along what they say—and don't forget to thank them for contributing to our class's learning!*

Explain to a parent or other adult that you and your classmates have been given some responsibility to choose a study topic. Tell the adult what you would like to study, and why. Invite any questions from the adult about your interest in the topic.

Then ask the adult what he or she would want to study, if he or she were in your shoes. Why does the adult find that topic interesting?

Take notes on the back of this page.

## NOTES

The topic I want to study next:

........................................................................................

........................................................................................

My reasons:

........................................................................................

........................................................................................

........................................................................................

The topic the adult would like it study, if he or she were in my shoes:

........................................................................................

........................................................................................

The adult's reasons:

........................................................................................

........................................................................................

........................................................................................

........................................................................................

## Comments

After you have completed
this activity, each of you
please sign your name and
the date below. If you have
any comments, please
write them in the space
provided.

........................................................................................

........................................................................................

........................................................................................

........................................................................................

**Signatures**                                                    **Date**

........................................................................................

Please return this activity to school. Thank you.

# Different Times

### Before Sending Home the Activity

This activity is useful for the end of a history unit, to consolidate students' understanding of the period and to show its relevance to their own lives. Ask students to think about what they know about living in the historical period they have just studied, and compare it to these times. What would be the advantages of living then? What would be the advantages of living now? What do the different times have in common? Have a whole-class brainstorm on the topic, and write students' ideas on the board in a Venn diagram (one circle labeled "Advantages of Living in _____" and the other labeled "Advantages of Living Now"). Then encourage discussion of the ideas in each part of the diagram, and add anything new that arises during students' conversation.

After some discussion, have students make their own Venn diagrams of the advantages of living in either time. Explain that they only need to use items that they agree with from the class diagram, and encourage them to add any other ideas that occur to them. Be sure students bring home their diagrams with their Home Activity sheet.

Before sending the activity home, ask the class for suggestions about making this Homeside Activity successful.

### Follow-Up

Invite volunteers to name the historical periods that adults would choose to live in, as well as the adult's thinking about what would be better and worse about living in that time. Write these on the board. What common themes do they see in the adults' responses? What advantages do we have living in this day and age that we all seem to appreciate? What's missing? What could be done about that? Or what makes up for that?

# Different Times

**Dear Student,**

*You are in charge of this Homeside Activity, which means you are in charge of finding an adult to do it with you, finding time you both have free to do it, explaining and "directing" the activity, making sure the adult signs it, and bringing it back to class. Please find about 20 minutes that you can spend on the activity with a parent or other adult—a neighbor, grandparent, older brother or sister, or family friend. If you'd like, get a bunch of people involved!*

*One of the most important reasons for doing this activity is that you and the adult will learn things from each other about what you think, feel, know, and want to know. In class we can then also learn from each other, when we share what we have learned at home. Just be sure to ask the adults for permission to pass along what they say—and don't forget to thank them for contributing to our class's learning!*

Tell a parent or other adult about the historical period you have been studying. Describe what it was like to live in that time. Tell the adult about the class discussion comparing that time to the present day. Show and explain your Venn diagram of the advantages of living in each time.

Then ask the adult what historical period he or she would like to live in besides our own. Find out the adult's reasons for this choice. Discuss what would be better or worse about living in that time compared to ours.

Take notes on the back of the page.

### NOTES

What historical era the adult would choose to live in:

.......................................................................

Why:

.......................................................................

.......................................................................

.......................................................................

What would be better about living in that time than in ours:

.......................................................................

.......................................................................

.......................................................................

What would be worse about living in that time:

.......................................................................

.......................................................................

.......................................................................

.......................................................................

## Comments

After you have completed this activity, each of you please sign your name and the date below. If you have any comments, please write them in the space provided.

.......................................................................

.......................................................................

.......................................................................

.......................................................................

**Signatures**                                      **Date**

_____  _____  _____

Please return this activity to school. Thank you.

# Famous

## Before Sending Home the Activity

Use this as part of a unit on poetry writing or in conjunction with a history, social studies, or current events unit that deals with the famous and powerful.

Ask students what they thinks makes a person famous. What kind of people become famous? How do they think it feels to be famous? Then read the poem on the following page aloud to students two or three times.

If possible, post the poem on butcher paper or project it on the wall. Discuss with students the poet's idea about what being famous can mean. How does it compare with students' ideas about fame?

Ask students to think about what personal characteristic they would like to be "famous" for, in the poet's use of the word. What do they know how to do that they are proud of? Are there ways they treat people that they are proud of? Give an example or two of your own. Then have students write a verse of their own to add to the poem by Naomi Shihab Nye, and have them copy it onto the back of their Home Activity sheet. Be sure to send home a photocopy of "Famous" with the activity sheet, too.

Before sending home the activity, ask the class for suggestions about making this Homeside Activity successful.

## Follow-Up

Have a whole-class conversation about how the activity went. Invite volunteers to describe what they would like to be "famous" for, or to describe any interesting ideas the adults had. Make a class poem titled "Famous," incorporating each student's verse.

## Famous

The river is famous to the fish.

The loud voice is famous to silence,
which knew it would inherit the earth
before anybody said so.

The cat sleeping on the fence is famous to the birds
watching him from the birdhouse.

The tear is famous, briefly, to the cheek.

The idea you carry close to your bosom
 is famous to your bosom.

The boot is famous to the earth,
more famous than the dress shoe,
which is famous only to floors.

The bent photograph is famous to the one who carries it
and not at all famous to the one who is pictured.

I want to be famous to shuffling men
who smile while crossing streets,
sticky children in grocery lines,
famous as the one who smiled back.

I want to be famous in the way a pulley is famous,
or a buttonhole, not because it did anything spectacular,
but because it never forgot what it could do.

—*Naomi Shihab Nye**

# Famous

### Dear Student,

*You are in charge of this Homeside Activity, which means you are in charge of finding an adult to do it with you, finding time you both have free to do it, explaining and "directing" the activity, making sure the adult signs it, and bringing it back to class. Please find about 20 minutes that you can spend on the activity with a parent or other adult—a neighbor, grandparent, older brother or sister, or family friend. If you'd like, get a bunch of people involved!*

*One of the most important reasons for doing this activity is that you and the adult will learn things from each other about what you think, feel, know, and want to know. In class we can then also learn from each other, when we share what we have learned at home. Just be sure to ask the adults for permission to pass along what they say—and don't forget to thank them for contributing to our class's learning!*

Talk with a parent or other adult about your classroom conversation about fame. Then read the poem "Famous" and explain the poet's different ideas about what it means to be famous.

Read the verse you wrote about a way you would like to be famous, and explain why you chose to write about that kind of fame. Ask the adult what characteristic he or she would like to be famous for, too, and his or her reasons.

Take notes on the back of the page.

**NOTES**

My "Famous" verse:

.................................................................................................

.................................................................................................

.................................................................................................

Why I chose to write about this kind of fame:

.................................................................................................

.................................................................................................

The personal characteristic for which the adult would like to be famous:

.................................................................................................

.................................................................................................

The adult's reasons:

.................................................................................................

.................................................................................................

.................................................................................................

## Comments

After you have completed this activity, each of you please sign your name and the date below. If you have any comments, please write them in the space provided.

.................................................................................................

.................................................................................................

.................................................................................................

.................................................................................................

**Signatures**                                                    **Date**

_____     _____     _____

Please return this activity to school. Thank you.

# Math Mentor

### Before Sending Home the Activity

Use this activity to help students consolidate and take pride in their mastery of a mathematical concept. After students have learned the concept, explain that they will be teaching it to a parent or other adult at home. Ask students for their ideas about how the concept relates to adults' lives, either in their jobs or at home. Then have a class brainstorming session about interesting ways to teach it—for example, a game, word problem, drawing, skit, hands-on demonstration, and so on.

Have partners work together to decide how to use one of the brainstormed suggestions. Give them time to practice teaching the math concept to each other.

Before sending home the activity, ask the class for suggestions about making this Homeside Activity successful.

### Follow-Up

Have a whole-class conversation about how the activity went. How did students like taking on the role of teacher? What was it like to teach math? What was it like to teach an adult? Do they have any suggestions for you as a teacher? Did teaching help them understand the math even better?

# Math Mentor

### Dear Student,

*You are in charge of this Homeside Activity, which means you are in charge of finding an adult to do it with you, finding time you both have free to do it, explaining and "directing" the activity, making sure the adult signs it, and bringing it back to class. Please find about 20 minutes that you can spend on the activity with a parent or other adult—a neighbor, grandparent, older brother or sister, or family friend. If you'd like, get a bunch of people involved!*

*One of the most important reasons for doing this activity is that you and the adult will learn things from each other about what you think, feel, know, and want to know. In class we can then also learn from each other, when we share what we have learned at home. Just be sure to ask the adults for permission to pass along what they say—and don't forget to thank them for contributing to our class's learning!*

Tell a parent or other adult about the math concept you are about to teach them. Explain how you think the concept will be useful to you and what it was like for you to learn it.

Then teach the adult how to do the math. Afterwards, ask the adult for any comments or questions. Is there anything more the adult would like to know? Tell the adult how you felt about teaching.

Take notes on the back of the page.

## NOTES

The adult's comments about the math lesson:

........................................................................................

........................................................................................

........................................................................................

........................................................................................

How I felt about teaching math:

........................................................................................

........................................................................................

........................................................................................

........................................................................................

How I felt about teaching an adult:

........................................................................................

........................................................................................

........................................................................................

........................................................................................

........................................................................................

### Comments

After you have completed this activity, each of you please sign your name and the date below. If you have any comments, please write them in the space provided.

........................................................................

........................................................................

........................................................................

........................................................................

### Signatures                                                Date

_____    _____    _____

Please return this activity to school. Thank you.

# In Character

### Before Sending Home the Activity

Use this Homeside Activity after students have done a lot of class or individual reading during the year, just to be sure they have a range of characters to consider for the activity.

Ask students to think about characters they have met in books they have read, either in class or on their own. (If students need help getting their thinking started, you might want to make a list with them of the books and characters they have encountered as a class.) Invite them to choose one character who is like them in some way—how they behave, how they see the world, what they enjoy, their worries, their family, a particular experience, or the like. What would they like to say to this character, if they had the chance? What might they talk about? Give them an example of your own, briefly describing how you are like a character in a book the class has read and what you would like to talk about with that character.

Have students note their chosen character and briefly list the reasons for their choice on the back of their Homeside Activity page. Then have students draft a short dialogue between the character they chose and themselves, and have them bring their final draft home with the activity sheet.

Before sending home the activity, ask the class for suggestions about making this Homeside Activity successful.

### Follow-Up

Have partners interview each other about the characters they are like and the characters the adults at home are like. Did they learn anything new or interesting about the adult? Bring the whole class together and invite students' comments about the activity. Ask for their ideas about what story characters can tell us. Can a character help us understand ourselves and others better? Why or why not?

# In Character

## Dear Student,

*You are in charge of this Homeside Activity, which means you are in charge of finding an adult to do it with you, finding time you both have free to do it, explaining and "directing" the activity, making sure the adult signs it, and bringing it back to class. Please find about 20 minutes that you can spend on the activity with a parent or other adult—a neighbor, grandparent, older brother or sister, or family friend. If you'd like, get a bunch of people involved!*

*One of the most important reasons for doing this activity is that you and the adult will learn things from each other about what you think, feel, know, and want to know. In class we can then also learn from each other, when we share what we have learned at home. Just be sure to ask the adults for permission to pass along what they say—and don't forget to thank them for contributing to our class's learning!*

Tell your parent about the book character that is like you in some way. Briefly describe the story the character appears in, too, to help explain the character and what you have in common. Read aloud your dialogue to the adult or, if you'd like, ask the adult to take one of the parts and read the dialogue with you.

Then ask what book, movie, or television character the adult thinks he or she is like. Find out why the adult thinks so, and take notes on the back of this page.

**N O T E S**

The character I am like:

.............................................................................................

How I am like that character:

.............................................................................................

.............................................................................................

.............................................................................................

.............................................................................................

The character the adult is like:

.............................................................................................

How the adult is like that character:

.............................................................................................

.............................................................................................

.............................................................................................

.............................................................................................

## Comments
..................

After you have completed this activity, each of you please sign your name and the date below. If you have any comments, please write them in the space provided.

**Signatures**                                                           **Date**

_____    _____        _____

Please return this activity to school. Thank you.

# School Year Summary

### Before Sending Home the Activity

This is a good activity to do in conjunction with an "end-the-year" activity. Before sending the activity home, ask the class for suggestions about making this Homeside Activity successful.

### Follow-Up

Have partners interview each other about their memories of the school year and the memories of the adults they interviewed. Encourage them to discuss any similarities and differences between their favorite memories and the adults' favorite memories. If they're the same, why might that be? If they're different, why might that be?

# School Year Summary

### Dear Student,

*You are in charge of this Homeside Activity, which means you are in charge of finding an adult to do it with you, finding time you both have free to do it, explaining and "directing" the activity, making sure the adult signs it, and bringing it back to class. Please find about 20 minutes that you can spend on the activity with a parent or other adult—a neighbor, grandparent, older brother or sister, or family friend. If you'd like, get a bunch of people involved!*

*One of the most important reasons for doing this activity is that you and the adult will learn things from each other about what you think, feel, know, and want to know. In class we can then also learn from each other, when we share what we have learned at home. Just be sure to ask the adults for permission to pass along what they say—and don't forget to thank them for contributing to our class's learning!*

Discuss this past school year with a parent or other adult. Review your favorite and least favorite memories of the year.

Then find out some of the things the adult remembers about your year in school. What is the adult's favorite memory?

Take notes on the back of this page.

### N O T E S

My favorite memories of my school year:

..................................................................................................

..................................................................................................

..................................................................................................

..................................................................................................

My least favorite memories of my school year:

..................................................................................................

..................................................................................................

..................................................................................................

..................................................................................................

Adult's favorite memories of my school year:

..................................................................................................

..................................................................................................

..................................................................................................

..................................................................................................

..................................................................................................

## Comments

After you have completed this activity, each of you please sign your name and the date below. If you have any comments, please write them in the space provided.

..................................................................................................

..................................................................................................

..................................................................................................

..................................................................................................

..................................................................................................

**Signatures**                                          **Date**

_____     _____     _____

Please return this activity to school. Thank you.

# Homeside Activities in Review

### Before Sending Home the Activity

Have a class discussion about how Homeside Activities changed from the beginning to the end of the year. How did they get easier? How did they get harder? What did students do to help make the Homeside Activities successful? What did parents or adult friends do to help make the activities successful? What were some favorite Homeside Activities? Explain this final Homeside Activity, and send home students' Homeside Activity folders along with it.

### Follow-Up

Invite volunteers to tell about the Homeside Activities they created. Students might also enjoy making a Homeside Handbook for future students, with suggestions for making Homeside Activities successful. Or, they might enjoy compiling a class book about Homeside Highlights that can be reproduced and taken home by students at the end of the school year so that they can share with each other the wisdom, experiences, and knowledge contributed by classmates' family members and friends. (If you reproduce actual finished Homeside Activities for this book, check with parents before sharing their contributions; an alternative would be to have students write about what they consider the Homeside Activity highlights and what they learned from them.)

# Homeside Activities in Review

## Dear Student,

*You are in charge of this Homeside Activity, which means you are in charge of finding an adult to do it with you, finding time you both have free to do it, explaining and "directing" the activity, making sure the adult signs it, and bringing it back to class. Please find about 20 minutes that you can spend on the activity with a parent or other adult—a neighbor, grandparent, older brother or sister, or family friend. If you'd like, get a bunch of people involved!*

*One of the most important reasons for doing this activity is that you and the adult will learn things from each other about what you think, feel, know, and want to know. In class we can then also learn from each other, when we share what we have learned at home. Just be sure to ask the adults for permission to pass along what they say—and don't forget to thank them for contributing to our class's learning!*

For this last Homeside Activity, talk with a parent or adult friend about some highlights of this year's Homeside Activities.

With the adult, look at the Homeside Activities from the entire year, and talk about the things you each did to make these activities successful.

Tell each other which Homeside Activities were your favorites. What did you like about these?

Then think of a topic or question for which you wish there were a Homeside Activity. Have a conversation about this topic.

On the back of this page, write a few sentences about the activity you created and what you and the adult discussed about it.

## NOTES

My new Homeside Activity:

........................................................................
........................................................................
........................................................................
........................................................................

What we discussed about this topic:

........................................................................
........................................................................
........................................................................
........................................................................
........................................................................
........................................................................
........................................................................
........................................................................
........................................................................
........................................................................
........................................................................

### Comments

After you have completed this activity, each of you please sign your name and the date below. If you have any comments, please write them in the space provided.

........................................................
........................................................
........................................................
........................................................
........................................................

### Signatures                                    **Date**

_____    _____    _____

Please return this activity to school. Thank you.

# ACTIVIDADES FAMILIARES

# Les presentamos las Actividades Familiares

## Querido alumno o querida alumna,

*Tú eres la persona encargada de realizar esta Actividad Familiar: te toca encontrar a una persona mayor que la pueda hacer contigo, hallar un tiempo que los dos tengan libre, llevar a cabo la actividad, obtener la firma y por último traer la actividad de vuelta a la escuela. Necesitarás hallar unos 20 minutos que puedas dedicarle a la actividad junto con uno de tus padres o con otra persona mayor: pudiera ser un vecino o una vecina, uno de tus abuelitos, tu hermano o hermana mayor, o algún amigo o amiga de la familia. Si quieres, ¡puedes reunir a todo un grupo!*

*Una de las razones principales por la cual realizar esta actividad es que cada uno de ustedes aprenderá mucho acerca de la otra persona: ambos aprenderán qué piensa, qué siente, qué sabe y qué quiere saber cada cual. Más tarde en la clase, seguiremos aprendiendo unos de otros al compartir lo que hemos aprendido en casa. Sólo asegúrate de pedirles permiso a las personas mayores para compartir lo que te han contado, y ¡no te olvides de agradecerles por su contribución a nuestro aprendizaje!*

Cuéntale a uno de tus padres o a otra persona mayor que este año escolar traerás a casa algunas Actividades Familiares.

Explícale que para realizar estas actividades, necesitarás conversar con él o con ella sobre algunos temas relacionados con tu trabajo escolar. Muéstrale a la persona mayor la carpeta que preparaste para tus Actividades Familiares, y háblale de tu diseño.

Conversen de cómo las Actividades Familiares serán distintas de otras tareas. Luego cada cual dirá qué es lo que quizá le guste de estas "tareas" de diálogo.

Escribe tus apuntes en el dorso de esta hoja.

## MIS APUNTES

Las formas en que las Actividades Familiares serán distintas de otras tareas:

.................................................................................................

.................................................................................................

.................................................................................................

.................................................................................................

Las cosas que quizá le gusten a la persona mayor de estas tareas de diálogo:

.................................................................................................

.................................................................................................

.................................................................................................

.................................................................................................

Las cosas que quizá me gusten a mí de estas tareas de diálogo:

.................................................................................................

.................................................................................................

.................................................................................................

.................................................................................................

### Comentarios

Después que hayan comple-
tado esta actividad, haga el
favor cada uno de firmar y
de escribir la fecha en el
lugar indicado. Si quisieran
hacer cualquier comentario,
por favor escríbanlo aquí.

**Firmas**                                                                      **Fecha**

_____        _____        _____

Por favor trae esta actividad devuelta a la escuela. Gracias.

# Las expectativas

### Querido alumno o querida alumna,

*Tú eres la persona encargada de realizar esta Actividad Familiar: te toca encontrar a una persona mayor que la pueda hacer contigo, hallar un tiempo que los dos tengan libre, llevar a cabo la actividad, obtener la firma y por último traer la actividad de vuelta a la escuela. Necesitarás hallar unos 20 minutos que puedas dedicarle a la actividad junto con uno de tus padres o con otra persona mayor: pudiera ser un vecino o una vecina, uno de tus abuelitos, tu hermano o hermana mayor, o algún amigo o amiga de la familia. Si quieres, ¡puedes reunir a todo un grupo!*

*Una de las razones principales por la cual realizar esta actividad es que cada uno de ustedes aprenderá mucho acerca de la otra persona: ambos aprenderán qué piensa, qué siente, qué sabe y qué quiere saber cada cual. Más tarde en la clase, seguiremos aprendiendo unos de otros al compartir lo que hemos aprendido en casa. Sólo asegúrate de pedirles permiso a las personas mayores para compartir lo que te han contado, y ¡no te olvides de agradecerles por su contribución a nuestro aprendizaje!*

Dile a uno de tus padres o a otra persona mayor lo que esperas de este año escolar. ¿Qué piensas que vas a disfrutar? ¿Qué retos piensas que vas a enfrentar, ya sea en lo académico o en lo social? ¿Qué crees que te ayudaría a tener éxito?

Luego pregúntale acerca de lo que le parecía difícil a él o a ella cuando tenía tu edad, ya sea en la escuela, en casa o en su trabajo. ¿Qué le ayudó a salir adelante?

Escribe tus apuntes en el dorso de esta hoja.

## MIS APUNTES

Lo que pienso que voy a disfrutar este año escolar:

..............................................................................................................

..............................................................................................................

Lo que pienso que me va a parecer difícil:

..............................................................................................................

..............................................................................................................

Lo que me podría ayudar a tener éxito:

..............................................................................................................

..............................................................................................................

Lo que a la persona mayor le pareció difícil cuando tenía mi edad:

..............................................................................................................

..............................................................................................................

Lo que le ayudó a la persona mayor a salir adelante:

..............................................................................................................

..............................................................................................................

..............................................................................................................

### Comentarios

Después que hayan completado esta actividad, haga el favor cada uno de firmar y de escribir la fecha en el lugar indicado. Si quisieran hacer cualquier comentario, por favor escríbanlo aquí.

..........................................................................

..........................................................................

..........................................................................

..........................................................................

**Firmas**                                                    **Fecha**

_____  _____  _____

Por favor trae esta actividad devuelta a la escuela. Gracias.

# Un mapa personal

## Querido alumno o querida alumna,

*Tú eres la persona encargada de realizar esta Actividad Familiar: te toca encontrar a una persona mayor que la pueda hacer contigo, hallar un tiempo que los dos tengan libre, llevar a cabo la actividad, obtener la firma y por último traer la actividad de vuelta a la escuela. Necesitarás hallar unos 20 minutos que puedas dedicarle a la actividad junto con uno de tus padres o con otra persona mayor: pudiera ser un vecino o una vecina, uno de tus abuelitos, tu hermano o hermana mayor, o algún amigo o amiga de la familia. Si quieres, ¡puedes reunir a todo un grupo!*

*Una de las razones principales por la cual realizar esta actividad es que cada uno de ustedes aprenderá mucho acerca de la otra persona: ambos aprenderán qué piensa, qué siente, qué sabe y qué quiere saber cada cual. Más tarde en la clase, seguiremos aprendiendo unos de otros al compartir lo que hemos aprendido en casa. Sólo asegúrate de pedirles permiso a las personas mayores para compartir lo que te han contado, y ¡no te olvides de agradecerles por su contribución a nuestro aprendizaje!*

Muestra tu mapa personal a uno de tus padres o a otra persona mayor. Para cada lugar que esté representado en el mapa, explica por qué lo decidiste incluir. Invita a la persona mayor a que te ofrezca comentarios y te haga preguntas sobre el mapa.

Luego entrevista a la persona mayor sobre lo que él o lo que ella incluiría si fuera a hacer su propio mapa. (Si lo deseas, invítale a que tome unos minutos para hacer su propio mapa.) Averigua los motivos que le llevaron a seleccionar cada lugar. Conversen sobre las semejanzas y las diferencias entre los dos mapas.

Haz tus apuntes en el dorso de esta hoja.

## MIS APUNTES

**Lo que la persona mayor incluiría en un mapa personal**

Lugar:

........................................................................................................................

Por qué incluyó ese lugar:

........................................................................................................................

Lugar:

........................................................................................................................

Por qué incluyó ese lugar:

........................................................................................................................

Lugar:

........................................................................................................................

Por qué incluyó ese lugar:

........................................................................................................................

Lugar:

........................................................................................................................

Por qué incluyó ese lugar:

........................................................................................................................

### Comentarios

Después que hayan completado esta actividad, haga el favor cada uno de firmar y de escribir la fecha en el lugar indicado. Si quisieran hacer cualquier comentario, por favor escríbanlo aquí.

**Firmas**                                                              **Fecha**

_____       _____       _____

Por favor trae esta actividad devuelta a la escuela. Gracias.

# Algo que cambió al mundo

## Querido alumno o querida alumna,

*Tú eres la persona encargada de realizar esta Actividad Familiar: te toca encontrar a una persona mayor que la pueda hacer contigo, hallar un tiempo que los dos tengan libre, llevar a cabo la actividad, obtener la firma y por último traer la actividad de vuelta a la escuela. Necesitarás hallar unos 20 minutos que puedas dedicarle a la actividad junto con uno de tus padres o con otra persona mayor: pudiera ser un vecino o una vecina, uno de tus abuelitos, tu hermano o hermana mayor, o algún amigo o amiga de la familia. Si quieres, ¡puedes reunir a todo un grupo!*

*Una de las razones principales por la cual realizar esta actividad es que cada uno de ustedes aprenderá mucho acerca de la otra persona: ambos aprenderán qué piensa, qué siente, qué sabe y qué quiere saber cada cual. Más tarde en la clase, seguiremos aprendiendo unos de otros al compartir lo que hemos aprendido en casa. Sólo asegúrate de pedirles permiso a las personas mayores para compartir lo que te han contado, y ¡no te olvides de agradecerles por su contribución a nuestro aprendizaje!*

Cuéntale a uno de tus padres o a otra persona mayor acerca del invento que crees que ha tenido el mayor impacto en nuestras vidas. Explica las razones que te llevaron a esa elección. ¿Cómo serían nuestras vidas si lo que elegiste nunca se hubiera inventado? ¿De qué manera viviríamos mejor? ¿De qué manera viviríamos peor?

Luego pregúntale qué piensa él o qué piensa ella que ha tenido el mayor impacto en nuestras vidas. ¿Cómo ha afectado ese invento su propia vida? Si pudiera elegir, ¿preferiría que existiera o que no existiera ese invento?

Haz tus apuntes en el dorso de esta hoja.

## MIS APUNTES

El invento que yo creo que ha tenido el mayor impacto en nuestras vidas:

.................................................................................................................

.................................................................................................................

Las razones por las cuales pienso así:

.................................................................................................................

.................................................................................................................

.................................................................................................................

El invento que la persona mayor cree que ha tenido el mayor impacto:

.................................................................................................................

.................................................................................................................

Las razones por las cuales piensa así:

.................................................................................................................

.................................................................................................................

.................................................................................................................

.................................................................................................................

## Comentarios

Después que hayan comple-
tado esta actividad, haga el
favor cada uno de firmar y
de escribir la fecha en el
lugar indicado. Si quisieran
hacer cualquier comentario,
por favor escríbanlo aquí.

**Firmas**                                                                              **Fecha**

Por favor trae esta actividad devuelta a la escuela. Gracias.

# ¿En qué lugar del mundo?

## Querido alumno o querida alumna,

*Tú eres la persona encargada de realizar esta Actividad Familiar: te toca encontrar a una persona mayor que la pueda hacer contigo, hallar un tiempo que los dos tengan libre, llevar a cabo la actividad, obtener la firma y por último traer la actividad de vuelta a la escuela. Necesitarás hallar unos 20 minutos que puedas dedicarle a la actividad junto con uno de tus padres o con otra persona mayor: pudiera ser un vecino o una vecina, uno de tus abuelitos, tu hermano o hermana mayor, o algún amigo o amiga de la familia. Si quieres, ¡puedes reunir a todo un grupo!*

*Una de las razones principales por la cual realizar esta actividad es que cada uno de ustedes aprenderá mucho acerca de la otra persona: ambos aprenderán qué piensa, qué siente, qué sabe y qué quiere saber cada cual. Más tarde en la clase, seguiremos aprendiendo unos de otros al compartir lo que hemos aprendido en casa. Sólo asegúrate de pedirles permiso a las personas mayores para compartir lo que te han contado, y ¡no te olvides de agradecerles por su contribución a nuestro aprendizaje!*

Habla con uno de tus padres o con otra persona mayor acerca del lugar que te gustaría conocer. Léele tu ensayo y contesta cualquier pregunta que él o que ella tenga acerca de tu interés por ese lugar.

Luego pídele que nombre algún lugar que le gustaría conocer. Pídele que te explique por qué le interesa tanto ese lugar. ¿Qué le gustaría hacer allí? ¿Por qué? ¿Qué le gustaría ver allí? Conversen sobre las semejanzas y las diferencias entre los lugares que han elegido. Luego conversen sobre las razones que llevaron a cada cual a elegir su lugar. ¿Qué razones comparten ambos? ¿Cuáles son distintas?

Escribe tus apuntes en el dorso de esta hoja y utiliza el diagrama de Venn que encontrarás allí.

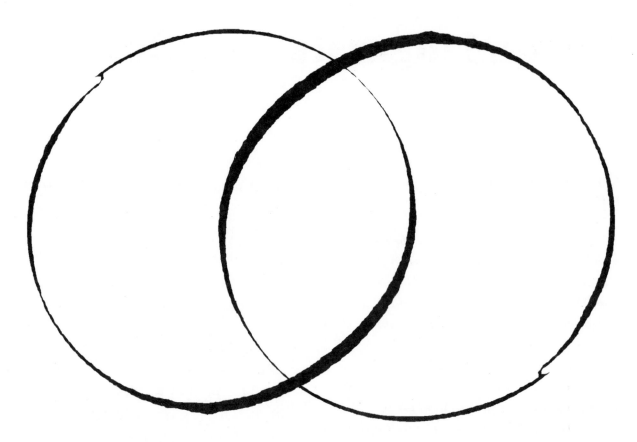

Por qué quiero conocer . . .                    Por qué la persona mayor quiere conocer . . .

........................................                    ........................................

## Comentarios

Después que hayan comple-
tado esta actividad, haga el
favor cada uno de firmar y
de escribir la fecha en el
lugar indicado. Si quisieran
hacer cualquier comentario,
por favor escríbanlo aquí.

**Firmas**                                                                    **Fecha**

_____    _____    _____

Por favor trae esta actividad devuelta a la escuela. Gracias.

# Poesía personal

## Querido alumno o querida alumna,

*Tú eres la persona encargada de realizar esta Actividad Familiar: te toca encontrar a una persona mayor que la pueda hacer contigo, hallar un tiempo que los dos tengan libre, llevar a cabo la actividad, obtener la firma y por último traer la actividad de vuelta a la escuela. Necesitarás hallar unos 20 minutos que puedas dedicarle a la actividad junto con uno de tus padres o con otra persona mayor: pudiera ser un vecino o una vecina, uno de tus abuelitos, tu hermano o hermana mayor, o algún amigo o amiga de la familia. Si quieres, ¡puedes reunir a todo un grupo!*

*Una de las razones principales por la cual realizar esta actividad es que cada uno de ustedes aprenderá mucho acerca de la otra persona: ambos aprenderán qué piensa, qué siente, qué sabe y qué quiere saber cada cual. Más tarde en la clase, seguiremos aprendiendo unos de otros al compartir lo que hemos aprendido en casa. Sólo asegúrate de pedirles permiso a las personas mayores para compartir lo que te han contado, y ¡no te olvides de agradecerles por su contribución a nuestro aprendizaje!*

Lee el poema "Expresión de sentimientos" a uno de tus padres o a otra persona mayor. (Encontrarás el poema en el dorso de esta hoja.) Luego describe la conversación que tuviste con tus compañeros sobre lo que dice el poeta (que un poema puede ser la expresión de tus sentimientos hacia una persona o un lugar, tratar de un sueño o de una meta que tengas, o hablar sobre cualquier cosa o experiencia, aún la más común y corriente).

Luego comparte con él o con ella el tema que has elegido para tu poema. Explícale los motivos de tu elección. Pregúntale qué escogería como tema si él o si ella fuera a escribir un poema.

Haz tus apuntes en el dorso de esta hoja. Más tarde, en clase, convertiremos nuestras ideas en poesía.

## Expresión de sentimientos

Si tan sólo estás dispuesto a buscar la poesía, la habrá:
mi alma, una pequeña motita, es mi guía.
El sol del atardecer y la hierba fragrante son cosas comunes y corrientes,
pero, con comprensión, pueden convertirse en un cantar glorioso.

—*Mei Yüan*
*traducido por Rosa Zubizarreta*

"Expression of Feelings VII" by Yüan Mei (4 lines, p. 69) from *The Penguin Book of Chinese Verse: Verse Translations by Robert Kotewall and Norman L. Smith*, edited by A. R. Davis (Penguin Books, 1962). Translation copyright © N. L. Smith and R. H. Kotewall, 1962.

### MIS APUNTES

Lo que yo pienso que sería un buen tema para un poema:

...................................................................................

Mis razones:

...................................................................................

...................................................................................

El tema sobre el cual la persona mayor escribiría un poema:

...................................................................................

Sus razones:

...................................................................................

...................................................................................

## Comentarios

Después que hayan comple-
tado esta actividad, haga el
favor cada uno de firmar y
de escribir la fecha en el
lugar indicado. Si quisieran
hacer cualquier comentario,
por favor escríbanlo aquí.

...................................................................................

...................................................................................

...................................................................................

...................................................................................

**Firmas**                                                                **Fecha**

_____    _____    _____

Por favor trae esta actividad devuelta a la escuela. Gracias.

# Una evaluación completa

## Querido alumno o querida alumna,

*Tú eres la persona encargada de realizar esta Actividad Familiar: te toca encontrar a una persona mayor que la pueda hacer contigo, hallar un tiempo que los dos tengan libre, llevar a cabo la actividad, obtener la firma y por último traer la actividad de vuelta a la escuela. Necesitarás hallar unos 20 minutos que puedas dedicarle a la actividad junto con uno de tus padres o con otra persona mayor: pudiera ser un vecino o una vecina, uno de tus abuelitos, tu hermano o hermana mayor, o algún amigo o amiga de la familia. Si quieres, ¡puedes reunir a todo un grupo!*

*Una de las razones principales por la cual realizar esta actividad es que cada uno de ustedes aprenderá mucho acerca de la otra persona: ambos aprenderán qué piensa, qué siente, qué sabe y qué quiere saber cada cual. Más tarde en la clase, seguiremos aprendiendo unos de otros al compartir lo que hemos aprendido en casa. Sólo asegúrate de pedirles permiso a las personas mayores para compartir lo que te han contado, y ¡no te olvides de agradecerles por su contribución a nuestro aprendizaje!*

Habla con uno de tus padres o con otra persona mayor sobre la conversación que han tenido en clase acerca de las evaluaciones escolares. ¿Qué les parece útil a ti y a tus compañeros de las evaluaciones? Al parecer de ustedes, ¿cuáles son las cosas que las evaluaciones no muestran de cómo les va en la escuela? Explícale a la persona mayor las categorías o los comentarios que te gustaría que se incluyeran en tus evaluaciones. Dile por qué piensas que esa información adicional le ayudaría a entender mejor cómo te va en la escuela.

Luego pregúntale a la persona mayor qué tipo de categorías o de comentarios le gustaría ver en las evaluaciones. ¿Qué es lo que le gustaría saber de cómo te va en la escuela que no se encuentra en la evaluación actual? ¿Por qué lo quisiera saber?

Haz tus apuntes en el dorso de esta hoja.

## MIS APUNTES

Las categorías o tipos de comentarios que me gustaría ver en mis evaluaciones:

........................................................................................

........................................................................................

........................................................................................

Mis razones:

........................................................................................

........................................................................................

........................................................................................

Las categorías o comentarios que le gustaría ver a la persona mayor:

........................................................................................

........................................................................................

........................................................................................

Sus razones:

........................................................................................

........................................................................................

........................................................................................

........................................................................................

## Comentarios

Después que hayan comple-
tado esta actividad, haga el
favor cada uno de firmar y
de escribir la fecha en el
lugar indicado. Si quisieran
hacer cualquier comentario,
por favor escríbanlo aquí.

................................................................

................................................................

................................................................

................................................................

**Firmas**                                                    **Fecha**

_____    _____    _____

Por favor trae esta actividad devuelta a la escuela. Gracias.

# Si pudiera, lo haría

## Querido alumno o querida alumna,

*Tú eres la persona encargada de realizar esta Actividad Familiar: te toca encontrar a una persona mayor que la pueda hacer contigo, hallar un tiempo que los dos tengan libre, llevar a cabo la actividad, obtener la firma y por último traer la actividad de vuelta a la escuela. Necesitarás hallar unos 20 minutos que puedas dedicarle a la actividad junto con uno de tus padres o con otra persona mayor: pudiera ser un vecino o una vecina, uno de tus abuelitos, tu hermano o hermana mayor, o algún amigo o amiga de la familia. Si quieres, ¡puedes reunir a todo un grupo!*

*Una de las razones principales por la cual realizar esta actividad es que cada uno de ustedes aprenderá mucho acerca de la otra persona: ambos aprenderán qué piensa, qué siente, qué sabe y qué quiere saber cada cual. Más tarde en la clase, seguiremos aprendiendo unos de otros al compartir lo que hemos aprendido en casa. Sólo asegúrate de pedirles permiso a las personas mayores para compartir lo que te han contado, y ¡no te olvides de agradecerles por su contribución a nuestro aprendizaje!*

Cuéntale a uno de tus padres o a otra persona mayor acerca de la conversación que tuvieron en la escuela sobre lo que les gustaría cambiar en el mundo. Cuéntale lo que tú elegiste, y las razones por tu elección.

Luego pídele a la persona mayor que elija una cosa que él o que ella cambiaría para mejorar al mundo, si pudiera. Pídele que te cuente los motivos por su elección. Conversen sobre las semejanzas y las diferencias entre sus dos elecciones.

Haz tus apuntes en el dorso de esta hoja.

## MIS APUNTES

Lo que yo cambiaría para mejorar al mundo (elige sólo una cosa):

..................................................................................................

..................................................................................................

Mis razones:

..................................................................................................

..................................................................................................

..................................................................................................

..................................................................................................

Lo que la persona mayor cambiaría para mejorar el mundo (elige sólo una cosa):

..................................................................................................

..................................................................................................

Sus razones:

..................................................................................................

..................................................................................................

..................................................................................................

..................................................................................................

## Comentarios

Después que hayan comple-
tado esta actividad, haga el
favor cada uno de firmar y
de escribir la fecha en el
lugar indicado. Si quisieran
hacer cualquier comentario,
por favor escríbanlo aquí.

......................................................................

......................................................................

......................................................................

......................................................................

**Firmas**                                                    **Fecha**

Por favor trae esta actividad devuelta a la escuela. Gracias.

# Momentos de reflexión

## Querido alumno o querida alumna,

*Tú eres la persona encargada de realizar esta Actividad Familiar: te toca encontrar a una persona mayor que la pueda hacer contigo, hallar un tiempo que los dos tengan libre, llevar a cabo la actividad, obtener la firma y por último traer la actividad de vuelta a la escuela. Necesitarás hallar unos 20 minutos que puedas dedicarle a la actividad junto con uno de tus padres o con otra persona mayor: pudiera ser un vecino o una vecina, uno de tus abuelitos, tu hermano o hermana mayor, o algún amigo o amiga de la familia. Si quieres, ¡puedes reunir a todo un grupo!*

*Una de las razones principales por la cual realizar esta actividad es que cada uno de ustedes aprenderá mucho acerca de la otra persona: ambos aprenderán qué piensa, qué siente, qué sabe y qué quiere saber cada cual. Más tarde en la clase, seguiremos aprendiendo unos de otros al compartir lo que hemos aprendido en casa. Sólo asegúrate de pedirles permiso a las personas mayores para compartir lo que te han contado, y ¡no te olvides de agradecerles por su contribución a nuestro aprendizaje!*

Cuéntale a uno de tus padres o a otra persona mayor acerca de lo que conversaron en la escuela sobre los momentos de reflexión. Cuéntale por qué crees que la gente a veces se detiene a reflexionar sobre su vida, especialmente en la época del Año Nuevo.

Lee a la persona mayor las ideas que tuviste cuando te pusiste a reflexionar sobre cómo ha sido este año escolar hasta el presente. Pónganse de acuerdo en una meta para tí (algo que los dos quisieran que tú lograras). Luego pónganse de acuerdo en una meta para la persona mayor.

Haz tus apuntes en el dorso de esta hoja.

## MIS APUNTES

Lo que celebro haber logrado en este año escolar:

........................................................................................................

........................................................................................................

Lo que quisiera que hubiera sucedido de otra manera:

........................................................................................................

........................................................................................................

Después de haber reflexionado, éstas son mis metas escolares para el año entrante:

........................................................................................................

........................................................................................................

Una meta mía para el año entrante, en la cual coincidimos (puede ser una de las metas que elegiste para tu respuesta previa):

........................................................................................................

........................................................................................................

Una meta de la persona mayor para el año entrante, en la cual coincidimos:

........................................................................................................

........................................................................................................

........................................................................................................

## Comentarios

Después que hayan comple-
tado esta actividad, haga el
favor cada uno de firmar y
de escribir la fecha en el
lugar indicado. Si quisieran
hacer cualquier comentario,
por favor escríbanlo aquí.

........................................................................

........................................................................

........................................................................

........................................................................

**Firmas**                                                     **Fecha**

_____   _____   _____

Por favor trae esta actividad devuelta a la escuela. Gracias.

# Mejoras

## Querido alumno
## o querida alumna,

*Tú eres la persona encargada de realizar esta Actividad Familiar: te toca encontrar a una persona mayor que la pueda hacer contigo, hallar un tiempo que los dos tengan libre, llevar a cabo la actividad, obtener la firma y por último traer la actividad de vuelta a la escuela. Necesitarás hallar unos 20 minutos que puedas dedicarle a la actividad junto con uno de tus padres o con otra persona mayor: pudiera ser un vecino o una vecina, uno de tus abuelitos, tu hermano o hermana mayor, o algún amigo o amiga de la familia. Si quieres, ¡puedes reunir a todo un grupo!*

*Una de las razones principales por la cual realizar esta actividad es que cada uno de ustedes aprenderá mucho acerca de la otra persona: ambos aprenderán qué piensa, qué siente, qué sabe y qué quiere saber cada cual. Más tarde en la clase, seguiremos aprendiendo unos de otros al compartir lo que hemos aprendido en casa. Sólo asegúrate de pedirles permiso a las personas mayores para compartir lo que te han contado, y ¡no te olvides de agradecerles por su contribución a nuestro aprendizaje!*

Pide a uno de tus padres o a otra persona mayor que trate de acordarse de cuando tenía tu edad. Pregúntale: "Si hubieras podido cambiar una cosa de tu escuela (o de tu trabajo) cuando tenías mi edad, ¿qué hubieras cambiado?"

Luego cuéntale qué es lo que tú cambiarías de la escuela si pudieras. Conversen sobre las semejanzas y las diferencias entre las respuestas de ambos, y por qué coinciden o difieren. Si tienes algunas ideas de cómo podrías lograr el cambio que quisieras en la escuela, también conversen acerca de ello.

Haz tus apuntes en el dorso de esta hoja.

## MIS APUNTES

Lo que yo cambiaría de la escuela si pudiera:

.............................................................................................................................

.............................................................................................................................

Mis razones:

.............................................................................................................................

.............................................................................................................................

Lo que podría hacer para empezar a lograrlo:

.............................................................................................................................

.............................................................................................................................

Lo que la persona mayor hubiera querido cambiar en la escuela (o en su trabajo) cuando tenía mi edad:

.............................................................................................................................

.............................................................................................................................

Sus razones:

.............................................................................................................................

.............................................................................................................................

En qué se parecen y en qué se diferencian nuestras respuestas, y por qué pensamos que es así:

.............................................................................................................................

.............................................................................................................................

## Comentarios

Después que hayan comple-
tado esta actividad, haga el
favor cada uno de firmar y
de escribir la fecha en el
lugar indicado. Si quisieran
hacer cualquier comentario,
por favor escríbanlo aquí.

.........................................................................................

.........................................................................................

.........................................................................................

.........................................................................................

**Firmas**                                                                                   **Fecha**

_____       _____       _____

Por favor trae esta actividad devuelta a la escuela. Gracias.

# Buenos deportistas, buenas personas

### Querido alumno o querida alumna,

*Tú eres la persona encargada de realizar esta Actividad Familiar: te toca encontrar a una persona mayor que la pueda hacer contigo, hallar un tiempo que los dos tengan libre, llevar a cabo la actividad, obtener la firma y por último traer la actividad de vuelta a la escuela. Necesitarás hallar unos 20 minutos que puedas dedicarle a la actividad junto con uno de tus padres o con otra persona mayor: pudiera ser un vecino o una vecina, uno de tus abuelitos, tu hermano o hermana mayor, o algún amigo o amiga de la familia. Si quieres, ¡puedes reunir a todo un grupo!*

*Una de las razones principales por la cual realizar esta actividad es que cada uno de ustedes aprenderá mucho acerca de la otra persona: ambos aprenderán qué piensa, qué siente, qué sabe y qué quiere saber cada cual. Más tarde en la clase, seguiremos aprendiendo unos de otros al compartir lo que hemos aprendido en casa. Sólo asegúrate de pedirles permiso a las personas mayores para compartir lo que te han contado, y ¡no te olvides de agradecerles por su contribución a nuestro aprendizaje!*

Entrevista a uno de tus padres o a otra persona mayor sobre el siguiente tema: ¿Tienen o no la obligación de dar un buen ejemplo para los jóvenes las estrellas del deporte? Pregúntale si había alguna estrella del deporte que él o que ella admiraba cuando tenía tu edad. ¿Piensa que hay estrellas del deporte hoy en día que dan un buen ejemplo para la gente joven? ¿Quiénes? ¿Piensa que las estrellas del deporte tienen más responsabilidad que otra gente famosa de dar un buen ejemplo para los jóvenes? ¿Por qué sí o por qué no?

Comparte tus propias ideas al respecto, y haz tus apuntes en el dorso de esta hoja.

### MIS APUNTES

Una estrella del deporte que la persona mayor admiraba cuando tenía mi edad:

.......................................................................................................................................

Sus razones:

.......................................................................................................................................

.......................................................................................................................................

Una estrella del deporte que la persona mayor piensa que da un buen ejemplo a la gente jóven de hoy en día:

.......................................................................................................................................

Sus razones:

.......................................................................................................................................

.......................................................................................................................................

La opinión de la persona mayor sobre si las estrellas del deporte tienen más responsabilidad que otra gente famosa de dar un buen ejemplo:

.......................................................................................................................................

.......................................................................................................................................

.......................................................................................................................................

## Comentarios

Después que hayan comple-
tado esta actividad, haga el
favor cada uno de firmar y
de escribir la fecha en el
lugar indicado. Si quisieran
hacer cualquier comentario,
por favor escríbanlo aquí.

**Firmas**                                                                           **Fecha**

_____     _____     _____

Por favor trae esta actividad devuelta a la escuela. Gracias.

# ¿Y ahora?

## Querido alumno o querida alumna,

*Tú eres la persona encargada de realizar esta Actividad Familiar: te toca encontrar a una persona mayor que la pueda hacer contigo, hallar un tiempo que los dos tengan libre, llevar a cabo la actividad, obtener la firma y por último traer la actividad de vuelta a la escuela. Necesitarás hallar unos 20 minutos que puedas dedicarle a la actividad junto con uno de tus padres o con otra persona mayor: pudiera ser un vecino o una vecina, uno de tus abuelitos, tu hermano o hermana mayor, o algún amigo o amiga de la familia. Si quieres, ¡puedes reunir a todo un grupo!*

*Una de las razones principales por la cual realizar esta actividad es que cada uno de ustedes aprenderá mucho acerca de la otra persona: ambos aprenderán qué piensa, qué siente, qué sabe y qué quiere saber cada cual. Más tarde en la clase, seguiremos aprendiendo unos de otros al compartir lo que hemos aprendido en casa. Sólo asegúrate de pedirles permiso a las personas mayores para compartir lo que te han contado, y ¡no te olvides de agradecerles por su contribución a nuestro aprendizaje!*

Explícale a uno de tus padres o a otra persona mayor que a ti y a tus compañeros de clase se les ha dado algo de responsabilidad para ayudar a decidir un tema de estudio. Cuéntale qué es lo que te gustaría estudiar, y por qué. Invítale a que te haga preguntas sobre tu interés en el tema.

Luego pregúntale qué es lo que le gustaría estudiar, si estuviera en tu lugar. ¿Por qué le interesa ese tema?

Haz tus apuntes en el dorso de esta hoja.

## MIS APUNTES

El próximo tema que quiero estudiar:

.......................................................................................................

.......................................................................................................

Mis razones:

.......................................................................................................

.......................................................................................................

.......................................................................................................

El tema que la persona mayor quisiera estudiar, si estuviera en mi lugar:

.......................................................................................................

.......................................................................................................

Sus razones:

.......................................................................................................

.......................................................................................................

.......................................................................................................

.......................................................................................................

## Comentarios

Después que hayan comple-
tado esta actividad, haga el
favor cada uno de firmar y
de escribir la fecha en el
lugar indicado. Si quisieran
hacer cualquier comentario,
por favor escríbanlo aquí.

.................................................................

.................................................................

.................................................................

.................................................................

.................................................................

**Firmas**                                                    **Fecha**

_____    _____    _____

Por favor trae esta actividad devuelta a la escuela. Gracias.

# Otras épocas

## Querido alumno o querida alumna,

*Tú eres la persona encargada de realizar esta Actividad Familiar: te toca encontrar a una persona mayor que la pueda hacer contigo, hallar un tiempo que los dos tengan libre, llevar a cabo la actividad, obtener la firma y por último traer la actividad de vuelta a la escuela. Necesitarás hallar unos 20 minutos que puedas dedicarle a la actividad junto con uno de tus padres o con otra persona mayor: pudiera ser un vecino o una vecina, uno de tus abuelitos, tu hermano o hermana mayor, o algún amigo o amiga de la familia. Si quieres, ¡puedes reunir a todo un grupo!*

*Una de las razones principales por la cual realizar esta actividad es que cada uno de ustedes aprenderá mucho acerca de la otra persona: ambos aprenderán qué piensa, qué siente, qué sabe y qué quiere saber cada cual. Más tarde en la clase, seguiremos aprendiendo unos de otros al compartir lo que hemos aprendido en casa. Sólo asegúrate de pedirles permiso a las personas mayores para compartir lo que te han contado, y ¡no te olvides de agradecerles por su contribución a nuestro aprendizaje!*

Cuéntale a uno de tus padres o a otra persona mayor sobre el período histórico que has estado estudiando. Describe qué has aprendido sobre la vida en esos tiempos. Cuéntale sobre la conversación que tuvieron en clase, en la que compararon ésa época con el presente. Muéstrale y explícale tu diagrama de Venn sobre las ventajas de vivir en cada época.

Luego pregúntale en qué período histórico le interesaría vivir. Averigua los motivos que le llevaron a esa elección. Conversen sobre las ventajas y las desventajas de vivir en esa época en lugar de vivir en la nuestra.

Haz tus apuntes en el dorso de esta hoja.

## MIS APUNTES

El período histórico en el que le interesaría vivir a la persona mayor:

........................................................................................................

Por qué:

........................................................................................................

........................................................................................................

........................................................................................................

Las ventajas de vivir en esa época en lugar de en la nuestra:

........................................................................................................

........................................................................................................

........................................................................................................

........................................................................................................

Las desventajas de vivir en esa época:

........................................................................................................

........................................................................................................

........................................................................................................

........................................................................................................

## Comentarios

Después que hayan comple-
tado esta actividad, haga el
favor cada uno de firmar y
de escribir la fecha en el
lugar indicado. Si quisieran
hacer cualquier comentario,
por favor escríbanlo aquí.

**Firmas**

**Fecha**

_____  _____

Por favor trae esta actividad devuelta a la escuela. Gracias.

# La fama

## Querido alumno
## o querida alumna,

*Tú eres la persona encargada de realizar esta Actividad Familiar: te toca encontrar a una persona mayor que la pueda hacer contigo, hallar un tiempo que los dos tengan libre, llevar a cabo la actividad, obtener la firma y por último traer la actividad de vuelta a la escuela. Necesitarás hallar unos 20 minutos que puedas dedicarle a la actividad junto con uno de tus padres o con otra persona mayor: pudiera ser un vecino o una vecina, uno de tus abuelitos, tu hermano o hermana mayor, o algún amigo o amiga de la familia. Si quieres, ¡puedes reunir a todo un grupo!*

*Una de las razones principales por la cual realizar esta actividad es que cada uno de ustedes aprenderá mucho acerca de la otra persona: ambos aprenderán qué piensa, qué siente, qué sabe y qué quiere saber cada cual. Más tarde en la clase, seguiremos aprendiendo unos de otros al compartir lo que hemos aprendido en casa. Sólo asegúrate de pedirles permiso a las personas mayores para compartir lo que te han contado, y ¡no te olvides de agradecerles por su contribución a nuestro aprendizaje!*

Conversa con uno de tus padres o con otra persona mayor sobre la conversación que tuvieron en clase sobre la fama. Luego lean el poema "La fama" y explica las distintas ideas que tiene la autora sobre lo que significa el tener fama o el ser famosa.

Lee el verso que escribiste sobre la manera en la cual a ti te gustaría tener fama, y explica el por qué de tu elección. Pregúntale a la persona mayor por qué cualidad le gustaría tener fama, y pídele que te explique sus razones.

Haz tus apuntes en el dorso de esta hoja.

**MIS APUNTES**

Mi verso sobre "La fama"

.................................................................................

.................................................................................

.................................................................................

Por qué quise escribir sobre este tema:

.................................................................................

.................................................................................

La cualidad por la cual le gustaría a la persona mayor tener fama:

.................................................................................

.................................................................................

Sus razones:

.................................................................................

.................................................................................

.................................................................................

## Comentarios

Después que hayan comple-
tado esta actividad, haga el
favor cada uno de firmar y
de escribir la fecha en el
lugar indicado. Si quisieran
hacer cualquier comentario,
por favor escríbanlo aquí.

.................................................................................

.................................................................................

.................................................................................

.................................................................................

**Firmas**                                                           **Fecha**

_____    _____    _____

Por favor trae esta actividad devuelta a la escuela. Gracias.

## La fama

El río tiene fama para el pez.

La voz fuerte es famosa para el silencio,
que supo que iba a heredar la tierra
antes que nadie lo dijese.

El gato que duerme sobre la cerca tiene fama para los pájaros
que lo observan desde el nido.

La lágrima es famosa, brevemente, para la mejilla.

La idea que guardas en el pecho
es famosa para tu pecho.

La bota tiene fama para la tierra,
más fama que el zapato de vestir,
que es famoso sólo para los pisos.

La fotografía arrugada es famosa para el que la lleva consigo
y no tiene fama alguna para la persona allí retratada.

Quiero ser famosa para los hombres que caminan arrastrando los pies,
que sonríen al cruzar la calle,
los niños pegajosos en la cola del mercado,
la fama de ser quien les devolvió la sonrisa.

Quiero ser famosa de la misma manera que una polea lo es,
o un ojal, no porque hizo nada espectacular,
sino porque nunca se olvidó de lo que podía hacer.

*—Naomi Shihab Nye\**
*traducido por Rosa Zubizarreta*

# Tutor de matemáticas

### Querido alumno o querida alumna,

*Tú eres la persona encargada de realizar esta Actividad Familiar: te toca encontrar a una persona mayor que la pueda hacer contigo, hallar un tiempo que los dos tengan libre, llevar a cabo la actividad, obtener la firma y por último traer la actividad de vuelta a la escuela. Necesitarás hallar unos 20 minutos que puedas dedicarle a la actividad junto con uno de tus padres o con otra persona mayor: pudiera ser un vecino o una vecina, uno de tus abuelitos, tu hermano o hermana mayor, o algún amigo o amiga de la familia. Si quieres, ¡puedes reunir a todo un grupo!*

*Una de las razones principales por la cual realizar esta actividad es que cada uno de ustedes aprenderá mucho acerca de la otra persona: ambos aprenderán qué piensa, qué siente, qué sabe y qué quiere saber cada cual. Más tarde en la clase, seguiremos aprendiendo unos de otros al compartir lo que hemos aprendido en casa. Sólo asegúrate de pedirles permiso a las personas mayores para compartir lo que te han contado, y ¡no te olvides de agradecerles por su contribución a nuestro aprendizaje!*

Cuéntale a uno de tus padres o a otra persona mayor sobre el concepto de matemáticas que le vas a enseñar. Explícale cómo crees que el concepto puede ser útil y cómo fue para ti el aprenderlo.

Luego enséñale a hacer ese tipo de matemáticas. Después, invítale a compartir sus comentarios o sus preguntas. ¿Hay algo más que quisiera saber? Cuéntale cómo te sentiste en tu papel de maestro.

Haz tus apuntes en el revés de esta hoja.

### MIS APUNTES

Los comentarios de la persona mayor sobre la lección de matemáticas:

.................................................................................................................

.................................................................................................................

.................................................................................................................

Cómo me sentí al enseñar matemáticas:

.................................................................................................................

.................................................................................................................

.................................................................................................................

Cómo me sentí al enseñarle algo a una persona mayor:

.................................................................................................................

.................................................................................................................

.................................................................................................................

.................................................................................................................

### Comentarios

Después que hayan completado esta actividad, haga el favor cada uno de firmar y de escribir la fecha en el lugar indicado. Si quisieran hacer cualquier comentario, por favor escríbanlo aquí.

.................................................................

.................................................................

.................................................................

.................................................................

**Firmas**

**Fecha**

_____     _____

Por favor trae esta actividad devuelta a la escuela. Gracias.

# Un gran personaje

## Querido alumno
## o querida alumna,

*Tú eres la persona encargada de realizar esta Actividad Familiar: te toca encontrar a una persona mayor que la pueda hacer contigo, hallar un tiempo que los dos tengan libre, llevar a cabo la actividad, obtener la firma y por último traer la actividad de vuelta a la escuela. Necesitarás hallar unos 20 minutos que puedas dedicarle a la actividad junto con uno de tus padres o con otra persona mayor: pudiera ser un vecino o una vecina, uno de tus abuelitos, tu hermano o hermana mayor, o algún amigo o amiga de la familia. Si quieres, ¡puedes reunir a todo un grupo!*

*Una de las razones principales por la cual realizar esta actividad es que cada uno de ustedes aprenderá mucho acerca de la otra persona: ambos aprenderán qué piensa, qué siente, qué sabe y qué quiere saber cada cual. Más tarde en la clase, seguiremos aprendiendo unos de otros al compartir lo que hemos aprendido en casa. Sólo asegúrate de pedirles permiso a las personas mayores para compartir lo que te han contado, y ¡no te olvides de agradecerles por su contribución a nuestro aprendizaje!*

Cuéntale a uno de tus padres o a otra persona mayor acerca del personaje de un cuento con el que compartes algún parecido. Describe brevemente la historia en la que aparece el personaje, para explicar mejor cómo es el personaje y en qué se parecen. Lee tu diálogo a la persona mayor. Si quieres, pídele que lea una de las dos voces y luego lean el diálogo juntos.

Después pregúntale con qué personaje se identifica. Puede ser un personaje de un libro, de una película o de un programa de televisión. Pregúntale en qué se parece a ese personaje, y haz tus apuntes en el dorso de esta hoja.

## MIS APUNTES

El personaje al cual me parezco:

......................................................................................................

En qué nos parecemos:

......................................................................................................

......................................................................................................

......................................................................................................

......................................................................................................

El personaje al que se parece la persona mayor:

......................................................................................................

En qué se parecen:

......................................................................................................

......................................................................................................

......................................................................................................

......................................................................................................

......................................................................................................

### Comentarios

Después que hayan comple-
tado esta actividad, haga el
favor cada uno de firmar y
de escribir la fecha en el
lugar indicado. Si quisieran
hacer cualquier comentario,
por favor escríbanlo aquí.

**Firmas**                                             **Fecha**

_____   _____   _____

Por favor trae esta actividad devuelta a la escuela. Gracias.

# Resumen de fin de año

## Querido alumno o querida alumna,

*Tú eres la persona encargada de realizar esta Actividad Familiar: te toca encontrar a una persona mayor que la pueda hacer contigo, hallar un tiempo que los dos tengan libre, llevar a cabo la actividad, obtener la firma y por último traer la actividad de vuelta a la escuela. Necesitarás hallar unos 20 minutos que puedas dedicarle a la actividad junto con uno de tus padres o con otra persona mayor: pudiera ser un vecino o una vecina, uno de tus abuelitos, tu hermano o hermana mayor, o algún amigo o amiga de la familia. Si quieres, ¡puedes reunir a todo un grupo!*

*Una de las razones principales por la cual realizar esta actividad es que cada uno de ustedes aprenderá mucho acerca de la otra persona: ambos aprenderán qué piensa, qué siente, qué sabe y qué quiere saber cada cual. Más tarde en la clase, seguiremos aprendiendo unos de otros al compartir lo que hemos aprendido en casa. Sólo asegúrate de pedirles permiso a las personas mayores para compartir lo que te han contado, y ¡no te olvides de agradecerles por su contribución a nuestro aprendizaje!*

Conversa con uno de tus padres o con otra persona mayor sobre el año escolar que estás completando. Conversen de tus recuerdos favoritos y menos favoritos de este año.

Luego averigua cuáles son algunas de las cosas que la persona mayor recuerda de tu año escolar. ¿Cuál es el recuerdo favorito de él o de ella?

Escribe tus apuntes en el dorso de esta hoja.

## ACTIVIDAD FAMILIAR

### MIS APUNTES

Mis recuerdos favoritos de este año escolar:

........................................................................................................

........................................................................................................

........................................................................................................

........................................................................................................

Mis recuerdos menos favoritos de este año escolar:

........................................................................................................

........................................................................................................

........................................................................................................

........................................................................................................

Los recuerdos favoritos de la persona mayor de mi año escolar:

........................................................................................................

........................................................................................................

........................................................................................................

........................................................................................................

### Comentarios

Después que hayan comple-
tado esta actividad, haga el
favor cada uno de firmar y
de escribir la fecha en el
lugar indicado. Si quisieran
hacer cualquier comentario,
por favor escríbanlo aquí.

### Firmas                                                    Fecha

_____

Por favor trae esta actividad devuelta a la escuela. Gracias.

# Repasemos las Actividades Familiares

## Querido alumno o querida alumna,

*Tú eres la persona encargada de realizar esta Actividad Familiar: te toca encontrar a una persona mayor que la pueda hacer contigo, hallar un tiempo que los dos tengan libre, llevar a cabo la actividad, obtener la firma y por último traer la actividad de vuelta a la escuela. Necesitarás hallar unos 20 minutos que puedas dedicarle a la actividad junto con uno de tus padres o con otra persona mayor: pudiera ser un vecino o una vecina, uno de tus abuelitos, tu hermano o hermana mayor, o algún amigo o amiga de la familia. Si quieres, ¡puedes reunir a todo un grupo!*

*Una de las razones principales por la cual realizar esta actividad es que cada uno de ustedes aprenderá mucho acerca de la otra persona: ambos aprenderán qué piensa, qué siente, qué sabe y qué quiere saber cada cual. Más tarde en la clase, seguiremos aprendiendo unos de otros al compartir lo que hemos aprendido en casa. Sólo asegúrate de pedirles permiso a las personas mayores para compartir lo que te han contado, y ¡no te olvides de agradecerles por su contribución a nuestro aprendizaje!*

Para esta última Actividad Familiar, conversa con uno de tus padres o con otra persona mayor acerca de algunos de los momentos especiales que hayan tenido este año con las Actividades Familiares.

Repasen juntos las Actividades Familiares de todo el año, y conversen sobre qué hizo cada cual para asegurar el éxito de las actividades.

Hablen sobre las actividades favoritas de cada uno de ustedes. ¿Qué fue lo que les gustó de esas actividades?

Luego piensa en un tema o en una pregunta que te gustaría explorar en una Actividad Familiar. Conversen sobre ese tema. En el dorso de esta hoja, escribe algunas oraciones acerca de esta nueva Actividad Familiar que acabas de crear, y de la conversación que han tenido sobre ese tema.

## ACTIVIDAD FAMILIAR

### MIS APUNTES

Mi nueva Actividad Familiar:

.........................................................................................................

.........................................................................................................

.........................................................................................................

.........................................................................................................

Lo que conversamos acerca de este tema:

.........................................................................................................

.........................................................................................................

.........................................................................................................

.........................................................................................................

.........................................................................................................

.........................................................................................................

.........................................................................................................

.........................................................................................................

.........................................................................................................

### Comentarios

Después que hayan comple-
tado esta actividad, haga el
favor cada uno de firmar y
de escribir la fecha en el
lugar indicado. Si quisieran
hacer cualquier comentario,
por favor escríbanlo aquí.

**Firmas**                                           **Fecha**

Por favor trae esta actividad devuelta a la escuela. Gracias.

# TEACHER SUPPORT MATERIALS FROM DEVELOPMENTAL STUDIES CENTER

### Among Friends: Classrooms Where Caring and Learning Prevail

In classroom vignettes and conversations with teachers across the country, this 202-page book provides concrete ideas for building caring learning communities in elementary school classrooms. With a focus on how the ideas of the research-based Child Development Project (CDP) play out in practice, Australian educator Joan Dalton and CDP Program Director Marilyn Watson take us into classrooms where teachers make explicit how they promote children's intellectual, social, and ethical development simultaneously throughout the day and across the curriculum. A chapter on theory and research provides a coherent rationale for the approach teachers demonstrate.

### At Home in Our Schools

The 136-page book focuses on schoolwide activities that help educators and parents create caring school communities. It includes ideas about leadership, step-by-step guidelines for 15 activities, and reproducible planning resources and suggestions for teachers. The 12-minute overview video is designed for use in staff meetings and PTO/parent gatherings to create support for a program of whole-school activities. The 48-page study guide structures a series of organizing meetings for teachers, parents, and administrators.

*The Collegial Study Package includes the book, the overview video, and the study guide. (Also available separately.)*

### Blueprints for a Collaborative Classroom

This 192-page "how-to" collection of partner and small-group activities is organized into 25 categories that cover the waterfront—from a quick partner interview to a complex research project. Over 250 activity suggestions are included for all elementary grades, in such categories as Mind Mapping, Deciding, Partner Reading, Editing, and Investigating. In addition, Fly on the Wall vignettes offer insights from real classrooms.

### Choosing Community: Classroom Strategies for Learning and Caring

In 9 videotaped presentations, author and lecturer Alfie Kohn describes pivotal choices that promote community and avoid coercion and competition in classrooms. A 64-page facilitator's guide for use in staff development accompanies the presentations, which include such topics as "The Case Against Competition," "The Consequences of 'Consequences,'" "The Trouble with Rewards," and "Beyond Praise and Grades." The package also includes Kohn's influential book *Punished by Rewards: The Trouble with Gold Stars, Incentive Plans, A's, Praise and Other Bribes.*

### Homeside Activities (K–6)

Seven separate collections of activities by grade level help teachers, parents, and children communicate. Each 128-page collection has an introductory overview, 18 reproducible take-home activities in both English and Spanish, and suggestions for teachers on integrating the activities into the life of the classroom. The 12-minute English overview video is designed for use at parent gatherings and staff professional development as an overview of a program of Homeside Activities; the Spanish overview video is specifically designed for parent meetings. The 48-page study guide structures a series of teacher meetings for collegial study.

*The Collegial Study Package includes six books (one each grades K–5), the overview video, the study guide, and a 31-minute video visiting 3 classrooms and parents working at home with their children. (Also available separately.)*

▶

# TEACHER SUPPORT MATERIALS FROM DEVELOPMENTAL STUDIES CENTER

### Number Power (Grades K–6)

Each 192-page teacher resource book offers 3 replacement units (8–12 lessons per unit) that foster students' mathematical and social development. Students collaboratively investigate problems, develop their number sense, enhance their mathematical reasoning and communication skills, and learn to work together effectively.

### Reading, Thinking & Caring: Literature-Based Reading (Grades K–3)

A children's literature program to help students love to read, think deeply and critically, and care about how they treat themselves and others. Teaching units are available for over 100 classic, contemporary, and multicultural titles. Each 3- to 10-day unit includes a take-home activity in both English and Spanish to involve parents in their children's life at school. Also available are grade-level sets and accompanying trade books.

### Reading for Real: Literature-Based Reading (Grades 4–8)

A literature-based program to engage the student's conscience while providing interesting and important reading, writing, speaking, and listening experiences. Teaching units are available for 120 classic, contemporary, and multicultural titles, and each 1- to 3-week unit includes a take-home activity to involve parents in children's life at school. Also available are grade-level sets and accompanying trade books.

### Reading for Real Collegial Study

Videotaped classroom vignettes illustrate key concepts and common stumbling blocks in facilitating literature-based classroom discussion. A 64-page study guide structures a series of 5 collegial study meetings that cover the following topics: "Reflecting and Setting Goals," "Responding to Students," "Handling Offensive Comments and Sensitive Topics," "Guiding Students' Partner Discussions," and "Assessing Student Progress."

### That's My Buddy! Friendship and Learning across the Grades

The 140-page book is a practical guide for two buddy teachers or a whole staff. It draws on the experiences of teachers from DSC's Child Development Project schools across the country. The 12-minute overview video is designed for use at staff meetings to build interest in a schoolwide buddies program. The 48-page study guide structures a series of teacher meetings for collegial study and support once a buddies program is launched.

*The Collegial Study Package includes the book, the overview video, and the study guide. (Also available separately.)*

### Ways We Want Our Class to Be: Class Meetings That Build Commitment to Kindness and Learning

The 116-page book describes how to use class meetings to build a caring classroom community and address the academic and social issues that arise in the daily life of the elementary school classroom. In addition to tips on getting started, ground rules, and facilitating the meetings, 14 guidelines for specific class meetings are included. The 20-minute overview video introduces 3 kinds of class meetings and visits a variety of classrooms in grades K–5/6. The 48-page study guide helps structure a series of teacher meetings for collegial study. In-depth video documentation shows 7 classrooms where students are involved in planning and decision making, checking in on learning and behavior, and problem solving.

*The Collegial Study Package includes the book, the overview video, the study guide, and 99 minutes of video documenting 7 classrooms. (Also available separately.)*